GIELGUD

GIELGUD

Robert Tanitch

London

FOR SYLVIA AND DONALD SNELGROVE

First published in Great Britain 1988 by
HARRAP LTD
19-23 Ludgate Hill, London EC4M 7PD

Copyright © Robert Tanitch 1988

ISBN 0–245–54560–3

Phototypeset by Falcon Graphic Art Ltd
Wallington, Surrey
Printed in Great Britain by
Butler and Tanner Limited, Frome

Also by Robert Tanitch

A Pictorial Companion to Shakespeare's Plays
Ralph Richardson, A Tribute
Olivier
Leonard Rossiter
Ashcroft

The author would like to express his deep
appreciation to Sir John Gielgud for all his
help and kindness.

Illustration opposite title page:
John Gielgud as Valentine in Love for Love *1944.*

CONTENTS

with contributions by
Lindsay Anderson   Harry Andrews   Peggy Ashcroft
Peter Brook   Gwen Ffrangcon-Davies   Dudley Moore
Laurence Olivier   Harold Pinter   Anthony Quayle
Dorothy Tutin   Charles Wood   Irene Worth

INTRODUCTION

John Gielgud is acknowledged by the acting profession, the public and critics alike to be one of the great actors of the twentieth century. This book is a pictorial record and full chronology of his career in theatre, film and television from the 1920s to the present day.

Asked in 1930 what he had learned most from his two seasons at the Old Vic (a period which established his reputation as the most promising actor of his generation) he replied 'teamwork'. His first concern always has been for the good of the company and he has surrounded himself with the most distinguished of actors and worked with the most influential and innovative directors, such as Theodore Komisarjevsky, Michel Saint-Denis, Harley Granville-Barker, Peter Brook, Lindsay Anderson and Peter Hall.

His classical seasons at the New, Queen's, Globe, Haymarket and Lyric Theatre Hammersmith – which included plays by Shakespeare, Obey, Chekhov, Sheridan, Wilde, Congreve, Maugham, Webster and Otway – were a National Theatre in embryo for which he has been given far too little credit in the post-war years. He not only brought Shakespeare back into the West End, he made him a commercial success. His productions set a standard by which future classical revivals were judged.

He has played thirty-two Shakespearian roles, one of them over 500 times. He has acted in plays by Ibsen, O'Neill, Shaw, Euripides, Molière, Seneca, Sophocles and created roles for Gordon Daviot, Noel Coward, Alan Bennett, David Storey, Charles Wood and Harold Pinter. He has directed some seventy productions, including three operas, one American musical (from which he was sacked) and over thirty modern plays.

He has played kings, prime ministers, popes, cardinals, diplomats, tycoons, schoolteachers, vicars (one demented) ghosts, three blind men and innumerable manservants and neurotics.

He has been cast as a secret agent, hospital administrator, surgeon, torturer, head of intelligence, chief of police, inquisitor, mandarin, viceroy, general, stockbroker, journalist, art-dealer, con-man, morphine-addict, incestuous father and concert pianist to a pierrot troupe. He has been in his time a butterfly, a Mock Turtle and a mole.

He has also been cast as an Arab quisling, Romanian count, Bulgarian buffoon, Austrian minister, Russian landowner, English knight abroad, Nazi scientist, Polish conductor, Danish prince and Texan evangelist.

He has played Shakespeare, Chekhov, Middleton Murry, and Julius Caesar three times. ('I don't think I'm a bit like Caesar really. They just think of someone with a big nose and a noble manner.') He has played himself.

He has travelled on the Orient Express, fought in the Crimean and Second Afghan Wars, and been murdered in Cairo, Rome, London and Denmark. He has committed suicide, hanging himself, shooting himself, and even cutting his wrists in a pornographic movie.

He has preached a sermon on hell-fire and damnation, confessed to a crime that has not been committed, slipped pessaries up his backside while drinking Chablis, and been found in a handbag in the cloakroom at Victoria Station (the Brighton line).

Arthur John Gielgud was born in London on 14 April 1904, the son of Frank Gielgud and Kate Terry Lewis. His father was a stockbroker while his mother was the daughter of Kate Terry, sister to Eileen, Fred and Marion Terry, a celebrated theatrical family whose beautiful voices and gift for tears he inherited. His paternal grandmother had also been a successful actress in Lithuania, famous for her roles in Shakespeare. He was educated at Hillside preparatory school (where he played the Mock Turtle, Humpty Dumpty, Shylock and Mark Antony) and Westminster.

At seventeen he decided to go on the stage. His parents were not keen; they wanted him to go to Oxford. He struck a bargain: if he had not succeeded by the time he was twenty-five, he would become an architect. By the time he was twenty-five he had appeared in sixty-six plays and was about to become the Old Vic Theatre's leading man.

In 1921 he auditioned for Lady Benson's Dramatic Academy and won a scholarship. While at the academy he walked-on as a soldier and played the English herald in *Henry V* at the Old Vic. He had one line: 'Here is the number of the slaughter'd French.' The following years, between terms, he walked-on in five more productions. 'I have been told,' he wrote at the time, 'that I was simply dreadful. I was weedy, and Lady Benson, a deft and amusing person and splendid teacher, said I walked like a cat with rickets.'

His first professional engagement was in 1922 in a long provincial tour of J.B. Fagan's *The Wheel* (starring his second cousin Phyllis Terry) in which he acted, understudied four roles and assistant stage-managed, all on a salary of £4 10s. a week.

In 1923 he won a scholarship to RADA and while still a student appeared in the West End as the poet-butterfly in the Čapek Brothers's *The Insect Play* and as an aide-de-camp in John Drinkwater's *Robert E. Lee*, in which he also understudied Claude Rains who was one of his teachers at RADA. His first role on leaving drama school was Charley Wickham in Brandon Thomas's farce *Charley's Aunt*, which he would direct some thirty years later with John Mills in the lead.

In 1924 at the invitation of J.B. Fagan he joined The Oxford Playhouse Company and over the next three seasons he was seen in eighteen roles, including Valentine in Congreve's *Love for Love*, Young Marlow in Goldsmith's *She Stoops to Conquer*, Marchbanks in Shaw's *Candida*, Naisi in Synge's *Deirdre of the Sorrows*, the Stranger in Ibsen's *The Lady from the Sea* and the Man in Pirandello's *The Man with a Flower in His Mouth*. His Trofimov, the perpetual student in Chekhov's *The Cherry Orchard*, which later transferred to London, was particularly admired by James Agate, perhaps the most important critic of his day and the one who would continue to champion his work during the next two decades.

In between the Oxford seasons he appeared as Romeo to Gwen Ffrangcon-Davies's Juliet, a performance many critics found unduly consumptive and effeminate, and which he himself thought 'pretty awful'.

He appeared in two more plays by Chekhov, an author with whom he would become increasingly identified, as actor and director, either in the genuine article or in the many pastiches which were so popular in the 1930s and indeed right up to the 1950s, and N.C. Hunter's *A Day by the Sea*. He was seen first as Konstantin in *The Seagull* and then as Tusenbach in *Three Sisters*, working for the first time with Theodore Komisarjevsky, one of the great influences in his career.

He understudied Noel Coward on two occasions: first in Coward's *The Vortex* and then in Margaret Kennedy's *The Constant Nymph*, taking over both roles, just two of the many highly-strung young men he would be called on to act over the next twenty years. He would later complain that authors only saw him in hysterical roles: 'You cannot imagine the number of plays dealing with neurotic poets.'

He appeared in a number of Sunday night and Stage Society performances before being rushed over to New York at the eleventh hour to replace the actor playing the Grand Duke Alexander in Alfred Neumann's *The Patriot*, arriving in time for the first dress rehearsal. He need hardly have bothered; the play was off after only eight performances. On his return he acted in Ibsen's *Ghosts*, playing Oswald to Mrs Patrick Campbell's Mrs Alving.

In 1929 at the invitation of Harcourt Williams he joined the Old Vic Company on a salary of £10 a week and stayed for two seasons. He played nineteen roles in all, fourteen of them by Shakespeare: Romeo, Antonio, Richard II, Oberon, Mark Antony, Orlando, Macbeth, Hamlet (in its entirety) Hotspur, Prospero, Antony, Malvolio, Benedict and Lear. He was also seen in Molière's *The Imaginary Invalid*, Pirandello's *The Man with a Flower in His Mouth*, George Colman's *The Jealous Wife*, and two plays by Bernard Shaw, *Androcles and the Lion* and *Arms and the Man*. In between seasons he found time to appear in Nigel Playfair's black-and-white Beardsleyesque production of Oscar Wilde's *The Importance of Being Earnest*.

Hamlet transferred to the West End. At twenty-six he was the youngest, finest, most musical and most spontaneous Hamlet many audiences had seen. He was praised for his intelligence, perception, grace and versatility: above all he was praised for his appreciation and faultless delivery of Shakespeare's verse.

There was therefore some disappointment that having just scaled Everest he should then appear in a poor part like Inigo Jollifant in an adaptation of J.B. Priestley's *The Good Companions*. His next play, *Musical Chairs* by Ronald Mackenzie, in which he was cast as a bitter and emaciated piano-strumming neurotic (predictably described by the press as a plain-clothes Hamlet), offered him far greater opportunities, while *Richard of Bordeaux*, one of his most famous roles, specially written for him by Gordon Daviot after she had seen his Richard II, established him as a West End star, putting him at the very top of his profession.

The roles which followed included the disillusioned schoolmaster in Ronald Mackenzie's *The Maitlands*, Hamlet again (his production ran for 155 performances in the West End, breaking all records for the play since Henry Irving) and André Obey's *Noah*, in which he was barely recognisable beneath his enormous white whiskers and vast shapeless garments.

He had been going to appear in his own and Terence Rattigan's adaptation of *A Tale of Two Cities* until Sir John Martin-Harvey, who had been playing Sydney Carton in *The Only Way*, off and on, for the last thirty-six years, complained that their production would jeopardise the success of his farewell tour. So the Dickens was cancelled and he appeared instead in *Romeo and Juliet*, alternating the lead-role and Mercutio with Laurence Olivier. This famous production, highly praised for its freshness, speed, continuity and also for its youth, was the definitive *Romeo and Juliet* of the 1930s and nothing comparable would be seen until well after the Second World War and Franco Zeffirelli's production with John Stride and Judi Dench at the Old Vic, the Kenneth Macmillan ballet with Rudolph Nureyev and Margot Fonteyn and the Leonard Bernstein-Stephen Sondheim musical *West Side Story*.

The Seagull, in which he played Trigorin, was the first full-scale production of a play by Chekhov in the West End and was by common consent the high-watermark of Theodore Komisarjevsky's achievement, famous for its poetic beauty and brilliant ensemble work. 'There is no play now running worthy to be mentioned in the same breath as *The Seagull*,' wrote Herbert Farjeon in the *Sunday Pictorial*.

He arrived in New York in 1936, the most eagerly awaited Hamlet since John Barrymore. He divided the critics as to whether he had surpassed Barrymore or not. (Those who thought he had not were those who wanted him to be more like Barrymore.) The production was a smash hit and broke Barrymore's record of 101 performances.

Returning to the West End, after an absence of nearly a year, and having had his fill of Shakespeare and wishing to appear in a new work, he chose *He Was Born Gay*, expecially written for him by Emlyn Williams, an unlikely story about the Lost Dauphin of the Temple, which was withdrawn after only twelve performances.

He then went into management with a season of four classical revivals, each with a limited and guaranteed run of not less than eight and not more than ten weeks, the first venture of its kind since the pre-First World War days of the Vedrenne-Barker management at the Royal Court Theatre. The plays were *Richard II*, *The School for Scandal*, *Three Sisters* and *The Merchant of Venice*; his roles were Richard, Joseph Surface, Vershinin and Shylock. The greatest success, artistically and financially, was *Three Sisters*, directed by Michel Saint-Denis, one of the great Chekhovian productions, and like Komisarjevsky's *The Seagull*, much admired for its poetic beauty and brilliant ensemble playing. 'Nothing I have seen in the theatre for many years', wrote A.E.Wilson in the *Star*, 'has so profoundly moved me and so burned itself into my memory.'

Keen to appear in modern dress after his classical stint and equally keen to be relieved of the burden of management he accepted the part of the elder son in Dodie Smith's golden wedding anniversary play, *Dear Octopus*, a cosy three-generation chronicle which ran very successfully for a year.

In 1939 he revived *Hamlet* at the Lyceum Theatre (the last production before it closed) and took it to Elsinore before returning to London to appear in *The Importance of Being Earnest*, which to this day is still regarded by many (even those who never saw it) as the definitive performance of Wilde's comedy.

The Old Vic, having gone dark like other theatres at the outbreak of the Second World War, re-opened with *King Lear* and *The Tempest*, the last production before the theatre was gutted in an air-raid in 1942. His Olympean Lear owed much to Harley Granville-Barker's *Prefaces to Shakespeare* and his inspirational rehearsals. His Prospero, scholarly and lightly bearded, looked as if he had just stepped out of El Greco's *The Agony in the Garden*.

His next appearance was in the old Gerald du Maurier role of the drunken artist in *Dear Brutus*, in which everybody is allowed a second chance, a characteristic bit of James Barrie whimsy which seemed even more unlikely at the height of the Blitz.

When *Macbeth* opened in London after a five month gruelling tour of the provinces, many thought his production superior to his performance. 'I have the wrong face for Macbeth,' he told Harold Hobson years later. 'The whole point about Macbeth is that he doesn't look like a man who would see ghosts. But I look as if I see ghosts all the time.'

He revived *The Importance of Being Earnest*; entertained the troops in Malta and Gibraltar; understudied the understudy at twenty-four hours notice in Shaw's *The Doctor's Dilemma* (playing Dubedat, a role he had not acted since RADA); and scored an enormous success in his own production of *Love for Love*, as Valentine. Alan Dent, writing in *Punch*, was ecstatic: 'Speaking after careful consideration and after viewing the whole thing from both circle and stalls, we should say that this is immeasurably the richest, the most satisfying, and the most Congrevian production of a Congreve play we have ever seen or are ever likely to see.'

Love for Love joined his Theatre Royal Haymarket 1944/45 season which included Somerset Maugham's *The Circle*, in which he gave a witty performance as the priggish husband, *Hamlet*, *A Midsummer Night's Dream*, as Oberon, and John Webster's *The Duchess of Malfi*, a play he disliked, in which he was cast as the neurotic Ferdinand.

He toured India and the Far East, entertaining the troops with Noel Coward's *Blithe Spirit* and *Hamlet* (he would have preferred to have taken *Charley's Aunt*). He came back to England, uncertain what he wanted to do, only certain that he did not want to do any more classics. He had planned to direct Robert Helpmann in Rodney Ackland's adaptation of Dostoyevsky's *Crime and Punishment*, but when Helpmann was advised by his doctors to rest, he decided to play Raskolnikoff himself. The production was something of a comeback for Gielgud, the crown he had worn for so long, as the accepted leader of his profession, having recently been seized by Laurence Olivier in a series of memorable performances with the Old Vic Company at the New Theatre between 1944 and 1946.

In 1947 he was seen on Broadway in *The Importance of Being Earnest, Love for Love, Crime and Punishment* and as Jason in Euripides's *Medea*. The critics and public liked him best in the Wilde.

On his return to London, he waited a year before appearing as Eustace Jackson in St John Hankin's *The Return of the Prodigal*, a role in total contrast to all the neurotic parts he had been identified with for so long, but this once-radical Edwardian comedy was as unsuccessful as it had been at its first performance in 1911, the critics underrating Hankin badly.

He had infinitely better luck with Christopher Fry's *The Lady's Not for Burning*. Many people had great difficulty in remembering when a poetry play had kept audiences laughing so continuously. The comedy was strong on Christian virtues, actually believing in the kindness of God and men, and coming down firmly on the side of life. None of these sentiments would appeal to a later generation of angry young men who, in the mid-1950s, would have confined the verse drama, along with the well-made play, to the dustbins — except, of course that the dustbins were already full, in use on the stage.

In 1950 at the invitation of Anthony Quayle he made his first and long overdue debut at Stratford-upon-Avon in four key roles: Angelo in *Measure for Measure*, Cassius in *Julius Caesar* (his waspish performance is fortunately preserved on film), King Lear, and Benedict in *Much Ado About Nothing* (one of his finest productions) which would prove so popular that he would fight 'the merry war' off and on for the next six years with three different leading ladies, Peggy Ashcroft, Diana Wynyard and Margaret Leighton. The following year he appeared as Leontes in *The Winter's Tale* in London and the production broke all records.

In his season of three plays at the Lyric Hammersmith he was a self-effacing Mirabell in Congreve's *The Way of the World* and a virtuoso Jaffeir in Thomas Otway's *Venice Preserv'd*. He also directed Paul Scofield in *Richard II*, a role many people thought he could still have played himself, though he did not find that this was the case when he came to do so shortly afterwards at a Festival in Bulawayo.

It had been announced that he would appear in John Whiting's *Marching Song*, but in the event he chose to direct an all-star cast in N.C. Hunter's *A Day by the Sea*, a mock-Chekhovian piece, dismissed by Kenneth Tynan in particular as 'an evening of unexampled triviality', which ran very happily for a year in the West End, providing him with his first success in modern clothes since the war.

He revived *Much Ado About Nothing* and was seen in his fourth *King Lear*, a disaster chiefly remembered now for its striking abstract scenery by the Japanese sculptor Isamu Noguchi, which acted the company right off the stage.

Six months after John Osborne's *Look Back in Anger* had opened at the Royal Court Theatre, changing the theatrical map decisively, he appeared in a new play. 'What does a great actor do when he has been waiting two years for a worthwhile part to turn up?' asked Donald Hatwell in the *Bristol Evening News*. He answered his own question: 'He gives up the search and appears in Noel Coward's *Nude with Violin*. This is the awful fate which has overtaken Sir John Gielgud.'

At Stratford-upon-Avon he acted for the third time in *The Tempest*: when the production transferred to the vast Drury Lane Theatre in London it was his incomparable speaking of the Epilogue, some twenty lines, which audibly hushed the audience and was responsible more than anything else for the cheering.

Anxious then to do a modern play before appearing as Cardinal Wolsey in *Henry VIII* at the Old Vic, he found himself in Graham Greene's argument for God, *The Potting Shed*, which he had turned down when it was first offered to him.

In 1958 he was seen in sixty cities in Canada and America in *Ages of Man*, his famous one-man Shakespearian recital, a splendid showcase for his talent, which would be a regular standby over the next ten years, winning him world-wide acclaim.

Back in the West End he appeared in a fez (Ralph Richardson appeared in his underpants) in Enid Bagnold's *The Last Joke*, a joke few people either saw or appreciated, least of all Miss Bagnold who was not amused by what the actors had done to her play.

He joined the Royal Shakespeare Company in 1961 to play Othello in Franco Zeffirelli's production and Gaev in Chekhov's *The Cherry Orchard*. The first night of *Othello* is unlikely ever to be forgotten by either the actors or the audience.

He was next seen playing Caesar in a lounge suit in Jerome Kilty's adaptation of Thornton Wilder's Roman correspondence course, *The Ides of March* (the critics were unanimous: Beware the Ides of March) before returning to one of his most celebrated roles, Joseph Surface in *The School for Scandal* when his production, which had opened earlier in the year, was recast.

The New York critics were baffled by Edward Albee's *Tiny Alice*, in which he played a lay-brother who had lost his faith. 'In such a play,' wrote Walter Kerr in the *New York Herald Tribune*, 'it is very easy for both author and audience to get lost.' So, too, for the actor. Following this traumatic experience he waited a year to find the right play before deciding on *Ivanov*, the first Chekhov play he had ever seen, in a production in the 1920s. The all-star West End revival drew the town but not its enthusiasm. *Ivanov* is not one of Chekhov's masterpieces, though there were some critics who ranked his performance in the title role with his Hamlet and Richard II.

When he made his much belated debut at the National Theatre in 1967 many people wondered why he had not appeared there before. The answer was very simple: he had not been invited. His parts included Orgon in Molière's *Tartuffe* and the title role in Seneca's *Oedipus* ('a fascinating experiment which didn't bring me much credit. I wasn't very good in it and the whole thing didn't really work'). He had also been going to act with Laurence Olivier in Ibsen's *The Pretenders* until Olivier's ill-health sadly led to the production being cancelled.

He scored a popular success as the Headmaster in *40 Years On*, Alan Bennett's first play, a deft mixture of satire and nostalgia. He was also seen, far less happily, as a world-famous humanist (a Bertrand Russell-like role) in *The Battle of Shrivings*, an exhausting three-hour-long debate by Peter Shaffer.

When Gielgud and Ralph Richardson appeared at the Royal Court Theatre in 1970 they caused much the same shocked reaction as Laurence Olivier had when he had appeared there in John Osborne's *The Entertainer* thirteen years earlier. The public was still not used to the idea of the theatrical establishment working for the English Stage Company. The muted tragedy of David Storey's *Home* was the nearest the two actors ever came to playing *Waiting for Godot* and their adroitness with Storey's small-talk and non-sequiteurs raised hopes – wishful thinking, really – that they might now attempt Beckett. The play was a major turning-point in his career, putting him firmly into the mainstream and creating an entirely new audience of young people. ('A pleasant surprise for an actor of my age.') Five years later when he and Richardson renewed their partnership in Harold Pinter's *No Man's Land*, he scored an even greater success as the failed-poet, perhaps his greatest character performance.

Twenty years after he had turned down the Gabriel Pascal film of Bernard Shaw's *Caesar and Cleopatra* ('It was silly of me. Claude Rains played it and made all that money.') he acted Caesar at the Chichester Festival Theatre. Back at the Royal Court he gave an endearing imitation of himself in *Veterans*, Charles Wood's witty and affectionate joke at his expense. He followed this with his fourth Prospero.

It seemed appropriate that having just been in *The Tempest*, Shakespeare's farewell to the stage, his next role should be Shakespeare himself in retirement at Stratford-upon-Avon; the only regret was that the role should be a bit of character assassination such as *Bingo* by Edward Bond, who was

John Gielgud as John Worthing in The Importance of Being Earnest *1942.*

not really interested in Shakespeare except as a means to knock the bourgeoisie.

In 1977 he returned to the National Theatre to play Caesar in a production of *Julius Caesar* most critics came to bury, Sir Politic Wouldbe (not a good part) in Ben Jonson's *Volpone*, and, more rewardingly, as a professor or archeology in Julian Mitchell's *Half-Life*, an abrasive conversation piece which transferred to the West End. There was talk of a chamber production of *King Lear* at the Cottesloe but, when he learned there would be an exhausting tour abroad as well, he withdrew.

Eleven years later, about to enter his eighty-fourth year, he was back in the West End with Hugh Whitemore's *The Best of Friends*.

Gielgud made his film debut in 1924 in the silent movie *Who is the Man?* cast as a morphine-addict, a role created in the theatre by Sarah Bernhardt, and which he followed five years later with the Edgar Wallace thriller, *The Clue of the New Pin*, playing the murderer. His first talkie was *Insult*, also based on a play, a now long-forgotten African colonial drama.

He repeated his stage role of Inigo Jollifant in J.B. Priestley's *The Good Companions*. It never was a good part and he wasn't very effective in it, though there were some critics who thought if he were properly exploited he could have the world at his feet. A career in the cinema was the very last thing Gielgud wanted in the nineteen-thirties. He loathed films: they were, he said, terribly boring, terribly difficult and terribly arduous.

Alfred Hitchcock tempted him back in 1936 with the role of Ashenden in *The Secret Agent* (a modern-dress Hamlet, so he said). It was not an experience he enjoyed; and he enjoyed it even less when, at the end of a long and exhausting day's shooting, he had to dash back to the Old Vic and act in *Romeo and Juliet*.

He didn't appear again on the screen until 1941 when he played Disraeli in *The Prime Minister*, a companion piece to Robert Donat's *The Young Mr Pitt*, both elder statesmen being dragged out of a long retirement to make boring speeches justifying the Second World War. His performance was a triumph of make-up over history.

Twelve years later he was seen in Joseph L. Mankiewicz's *Julius Caesar*, repeating his stage Cassius. The film surprised everybody by doing better business than *Quo Vadis?*. His meticulous diction and classic profile were much admired on both sides of the Atlantic. 'I still loathe filming,' he said, 'it's not essential to me. It's a superfluous risk.'

He made a fleeting but memorable appearance in Laurence Olivier's *Richard III* as Clarence, a role which in most hands is usually no more than an advertisement for the efficacy of Malmsey wine. He appeared briefly, as everybody else did, in Mike Todd's spot-the-star spectacular, *Around the World in Eighty Days*, playing the first of his many manservants.

He played the heavy father in the ponderous remake of *The Barretts of Wimpole Street*, where the incest was so tactful the censor didn't even notice it. He was in the ill-fated Otto Preminger-Jean Seberg *Saint Joan*, playing a supercilious and much-edited Warwick. He had the rewarding cameo role of the French King in the Richard Burton-Peter O'Toole *Becket* and acted it with polished insolence. He was also in Orson Welles's *Chimes at Midnight*, playing Henry IV, one of his best screen parts.

He made two films for Tony Richardson: first the travesty of Evelyn Waugh's *The Loved One*, more Richardson than Waugh ('I couldn't bear it,' he said, 'it wasn't a funny film. It was just unpleasant'), and then in the mock-heroic, anti-war *The Charge of the Light Brigade*, as a fussing, absent-minded, old-maidish Lord Cardigan, a major turning-point in his career and his attitude to filming. Suddenly as if making up for lost time (and lost money) he seemed to be in everything. Films were no longer superfluous. He now made them as indiscriminately as he saw them.

He was Head of Intelligence in *Sebastian*, the dying Pope in *The Shoes of the Fisherman*, the Headmaster in *Aces High*, and the Austrian Minister in *Oh! What A Lovely War*, the last three roles barely extending beyond the credit titles. He had something better in *Eagle in a Cage*, playing a rude old Regency rake, and something infinitely worse in the musical remake of *Lost Horizon*, which he described as 'a pretty awful experience'.

He was cast as assorted ruthless tycoons in *Assignment to Kill, 11 Harrowhouse* and *Gold*. (He had once said he could never play tycoons.) He was the Chief Constable in *Frankenstein: The True Story*, the murdered man's valet in *Murder on the Orient Express*, the bigoted Old Cardinal in *Galileo*, the bumbling pimply surgeon in *Joseph Andrews*, and the hell-fire-and-damnation preacher in Joseph Strick's boring attempt to screen James Joyce's *A Portrait of the Artist as a Young Man*.

He was seen as Lord Salisbury in *Murder by Decree*, Carr Gomm in *The Elephant Man*, Lord Irwin in *Gandhi*, and a fictional anti-semetic Cambridge don in the award-winning *Chariots of Fire*.

He played the Polish émigré conductor in Andrzej Wajda's *Dyrygent*, one of his best screen performances, and many people at the Berlin Film Festival thought he would win the prize for the best actor; but in the event the award went to his co-star.

He was in the ultimate porno-flick *Caligula*, which had enough erections to build Rome in a day, and in *Omar Mukhtar – Lion of the Desert*, playing an Arab quisling hiding behind an enormous white beard. He played the Cairo antique dealer who gets his throat cut early on in *Sphinx* ('Actors who disappear quickly in this film should consider themselves lucky,' wrote Arthur Thirkell in the *Daily Mail*), and also the frosty, bible-quoting old retainer who gets poisoned in an unnecessary and unpleasant remake of *The Wicked Lady*.

He was the diplomat who resigned during the Suez crisis in *Plenty*, the animal rights campaigner in *The Shooting Party* and the KGB mole in *The Whistle Blower*. Some films like *Invitation to the Wedding, Scandalous, Priest of Love* and *Leave All Fair* were off before anybody knew they were on.

Arthur was a major turning-point in his career. 'If he doesn't get the Oscar nod for the best supporting actor there ain't no justice,' wrote *Playboy* magazine. He got the Oscar, the combination of English hauteur and deadpan crudity proving irresistible to the judges. The film, a smash hit in the United States, made him an international star.

His best screen performance, however, remains his full-length portrait of a dying author in Alain Resnais's *Providence*, described by him as the most exciting film he has ever made. Resnais's characteristic bit of visual legerdemain is Gielgud's long night's journey into day.

Over the last twenty years there has been talk of his filming *The Tempest* with Akira Kurosawa, Ingmar Bergman, Hiroshi Teshigahara, and Richard Attenborough with Benjamin Britten. *The Tempest* remains the one film he would still most like to do.

Gielgud made his television debut in America in 1959 as the failed schoolmaster in Terence Rattigan's *The Browning Version*, and his debut in England as the failed diplomat in N.C. Hunter's *A Day by the Sea*, a role he already had played for a year on the London stage. There was some regret about the Hunter, partly because of his unadventurousness but mainly because it was nothing like as good as the original production. The Rattigan, on the other hand, was a big success, winning universal acclaim.

He played the lustful Count in *The Rehearsal* (Jean Anouilh's *Les Liaisons Dangereuses* as written by Marivaux) and the Mock Turtle in Jonathan Miller's controversial, all too-human version of *Alice in Wonderland* deemed by the BBC to be unsuitable for children. He played Chekhov in *From Chekhov with Love*, adapted and staged by Jonathan Miller, in a series of tableaux based on the correspondence to and from the Russian dramatist.

He appeared in three plays by Bernard Shaw. 'You know the trouble with Shaw', he was quoted as saying in the *Radio Times*, 'is that all the characters have a gift of the gab. Now that he's dead I do think it would be doing everyone a service if many of his plays were drastically cut.' *Saint Joan* was cut to 140 minutes and, as the Inquisitor, he lost three quarters of his virtuoso speech. *In Good King Charles's Golden Days* would have benefitted from such cutting; the conversation went on for ever. He played Charles II (Charles I would have been better casting, of course, but a bit difficult since he does not appear in the play.) He was also Captain Shotover in *Heartbreak House*, an even more unlikely role.

He was seen in an adaptation of two stage productions, *Ivanov* with Claire Bloom, and *The Cherry Orchard* with Peggy Ashcroft, and in two original television screenplays, *The Mayfly and the Frog*, a bit of English whimsy with Felicity Kendall, and *The Love Song of Barney Kempinski*, a surrealist cartoon of New York with Alan Arkin, a pilot for a series which never got made.

He was the Writer in Friedrich Durrenmatt's allegory of Death, *Conversation at Night* ('an old piece of Swiss cheese, more holes than nourishment,' according to the *Sunday Times*) and the Caliph in James Elroy Flecker's *Hassan* (described by the *Observer* as 'skilful porn masquerading as a philosophical fable').

He was seen as Disraeli in *Edward VII* (a role not nearly so glamorous as the one he had played in *The Prime Minister*), as the Grand Inquisitor in Dostoyevsky's *The Brothers Karamazov* ('He spoke like God's own catechist,' wrote one critic) and as Lord Henry Wotton in Oscar Wilde's *The Picture of Dorian Gray*.

In the 1980s Gielgud spent much of his time in Agatha Christie murder mysteries and Roald Dahl's tales of the unexpected. He also made such blockbusters as *Les Misérables*, *The Hunchback of Notre Dame* ('Sir John Gielgud selflessly contributed the cameo appearance by Sir John Gielgud without which no costume or classic epic can hope to be sold to America,' wrote Philip Purser in the *Sunday Telegraph*), *Frankenstein*, *Camille*, *The Master of Ballantrae*, *The Far Pavilions* (The *Gone with the Wind* of India) and *Marco Polo*.

More recently he has been seen in Albert Speer Snr's *Inside The Third Reich*, Molly Keane's *Time After Time*, Sophocles' *Theban Plays* (playing Teiresias) Simon Gray's *Quartermaine's Terms* and Oscar Wilde's *The Canterville Ghost*.

His most famous television role remains Edward Ryder in John Mortimer's exceptionally faithful adaptation of Evelyn Waugh's *Brideshead Revisited*. His performance as the insufferable father (based on Waugh's own father) was one of his most vivid and memorable comic characterisations. Ryder was a comparatively small part, but Gielgud came to dominate the production, and the serial never really survived his early departure after the fifth episode.

John Gielgud, a classical, romantic and modern actor, equally adept in comedy and tragedy, has been one of the great influences on the theatre in the twentieth century. The profession owes him an enormous debt. The pages which follow are a record of his career, a testament to his virtuoso talent, scholarship, taste, wit and authority. They are also a tribute to the man himself, whose politeness, charm, proverbial unselfishness and perennial youthfulness and enthusiasm have made him one of the best-loved actors of our time.

1920s

John Geilgud as Felix in The Insect Play *1923.*

AS YOU LIKE IT – 1922

John Gielgud as Orlando in Shakespeare's As You Like It, directed by Oliver Bell and Hugh McNeill. This amateur production was seen at St Leonards, Rye and Battle. Gielgud is sitting in the front row, third from right.

THE INSECT PLAY – 1923

Algernon West, F. Kingsley Peile, Noelle Sonning, Anne Hyton and John Gielgud as the butterflies in Karel and Josef Čapek's The Insect Play, *directed by Nigel Playfair at the Regent Theatre.*

T HIS FAMOUS Czech satire opens with the flirting, fox-trotting butterflies; their sexual activities were severely curtailed in the English translation.

Gielgud played Felix, the poet butterfly, a pale and tragic figure who dies. In his white shirt, white flannels, golden battledore, wearing a green laurel wreath and carrying a shuttlecock, he looked very pretty.

I am surprised that the audience did not throw things at me.
JOHN GIELGUD *EARLY STAGES*

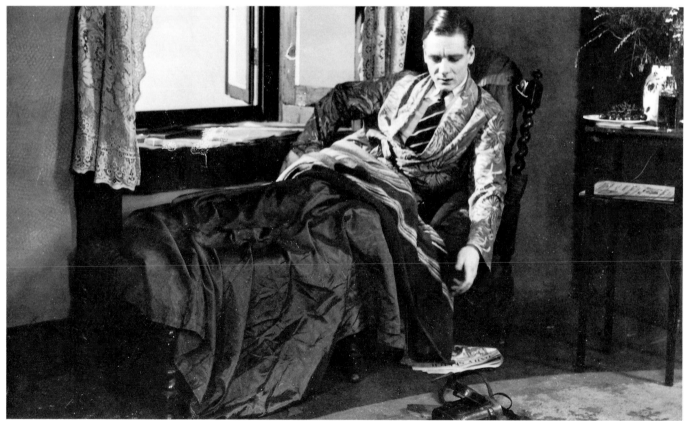

ROBERT E. LEE – 1923

Claude Rains as David Peel, John Gielgud as an aide to General Lee, Felix Aylmer as Robert E. Lee and Tristan Rawson as Tom Buchanan in John Drinkwater's Robert E. Lee, *directed by Nigel Playfair and John Drinkwater at the Regent Theatre.*

GIELGUD also understudied Claude Rains and played Peel, the philosopher-sniper, on three occasions.

WHO IS THE MAN? – 1924

John Gielgud as Daniel Arnault in Who is the Man?, *a silent film directed by Walter Summers.*

WHO IS THE MAN? was an adaptation of *Daniel*, a play specially written for Sarah Bernhardt by her godson Louis Verneuil.

Daniel is a young morphine-addicted sculptor who swears he is a woman's lover (when he is not) and is given such a tremendous thrashing by her irate husband that he dies. Gielgud thought he was terrible.

ROMEO AND JULIET – 1924

Gwen Ffrangcon-Davies as Juliet and John Gielgud as Romeo in Shakespeare's Romeo and Juliet, *directed by H.K. Ayliff at the Regent Theatre.*

AT NINETEEN Gielgud was the right age to play Romeo, but he didn't have the experience and, in his own words, 'made a frightful mess of it,' his passion often becoming mere hysteria. Nor was his self-indulgent performance improved by a wig and costume which made him look unduly effeminate. Gwen Ffrangcon-Davies got all the praise, he the brickbats.

Mr Gielgud has a good voice, a pleasant face and useful figure. He comes, they tell me, of a great theatrical family so he should be useful in the theatre in time. It was unfair to him to cast him for a public performance of Romeo. But it was most unfair to the young actors who have qualified to tackle the part, and most unfair still to the public. Mr Gielgud's body from his hips down never meant anything throughout the evening. He has the most meaningless legs imaginable.

IVOR BROWN *THE NEW AGE*

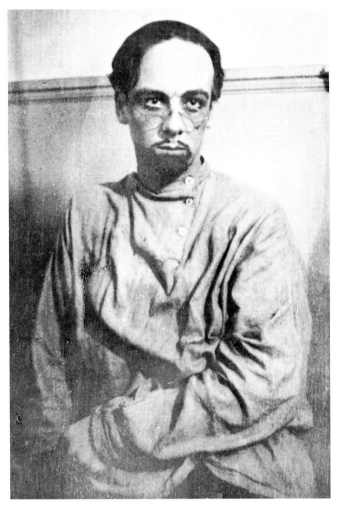

THE CHERRY ORCHARD – 1925

On the left John Gielgud as Trofimov in Anton Chekhov's The Cherry Orchard, *directed by J.B. Fagan at The Playhouse, Oxford. The production transferred to London, first to the Lyric Theatre, Hammersmith, and then to the Royalty Theatre.*

AUDIENCES AND CRITICS, unused to Chekhov, were divided as to the merits of the play. There were those who thought *The Cherry Orchard* 'flawless in artistic form' and 'an oasis just now in a desert of jazz'; equally there were many who found the play 'dull, stupid stuff' and saw 'no reason why this fatuous drivel should be translated at all'.

Gielgud, whose performance was much admired, has said that this was the first time on stage that he became someone other than himself. He modelled his make-up on his brother, Val.

Mr John Gielgud's Perpetual Student was perfection itself.
JAMES AGATE *SUNDAY TIMES*

THREE SISTERS – 1926

John Gielgud as Tusenbach and Beatrix Thomson as Irina in Anton Chekhov's Three Sisters, *directed by Theodore Komisarjevsky at the Barnes Theatre.*

DESMOND MACCARTHY, writing in the *New Statesman and Nation*, thought Gielgud was much too much the *jeune premier*: 'an ugly man had been transformed into a neurotic Adonis who might well have fascinated Irina.'

THE SEAGULL – 1925

John Gielgud (seated at table) as Konstantin in Anton Chekhov's
The Seagull, *directed by A.E. Filmer at the Little Theatre.*

*Mr John Gielgud, as the boy writer, proved once more that
he is unequalled as an English interpreter of Russian
drama.*
N.G. ROYDE-SMITH *THE OUTLOOK*

*The part of the young author was well played by Mr John
Gielgud, who should, of course, be playing Hamlet, and
was, in fact, doing so in this piece without knowing it.*
SIR TOPAZ *EVE*

THE CONSTANT NYMPH – 1926

*John Gielgud as Lewis Dodd in Margaret Kennedy and Basil
Dean's* The Constant Nymph, *directed by Basil Dean at the
New Theatre.*

DODD was a musical genius who spent much of his
time strumming the piano and making facetious
remarks. It was a role which Basil Dean had promised to
Gielgud but given to Noel Coward. When Coward became ill, less than three weeks after the play had opened,
Gielgud (who had been understudying Coward) took
over the part and played Dodd for the rest of a fourteen-
month run.

THE GREAT GOD BROWN – 1927

*John Gielgud as Dion Anthony and Mary Clare as Cybel in
Eugene O'Neill's* The Great God Brown, *directed by Peter
Godfrey, for the Stage Society, at the Strand Theatre.*

THE GREAT GOD BROWN is a philosophical drama with
masks. Dion Anthony, who is both Dionysus and St
Anthony, represents the conflict between 'the creative
pagan acceptance of life' and 'the masochistic life-
denying spirit of Christianity'. Dion's wife, who is repel-
led by his real self, accepts him only when he is wearing
the mask of Pan.

*Mr John Gielgud as Dion gave both sides of the character
and his frequent transitions from one to the other were
made with remarkable skill.*
MANCHESTER GUARDIAN

GHOSTS – 1928

Mrs Patrick Campbell as Mrs Alving and John Gielgud as Oswald in Henrik Ibsen's Ghosts, *directed by Peter Godfrey at Wyndham's Theatre. The production transferred to the Arts Theatre.*

Ghosts, which was revived in a series of special matinées to celebrate Ibsen's birth, would be the last time Gielgud would appear in a play by the Norwegian playwright.

HOLDING OUT THE APPLE – 1928

Hermione Baddeley as Vera and John Gielgud as Dr Gerald Marlowe in B. Wynne-Bower's Holding Out the Apple, *directed by Leon M. Lion at the Globe Theatre.*

Holding Out the Apple – the first time Gielgud saw his name in lights – was about a woman trying to conceal the fact that she had had one of her teeth knocked out.

The author described her play as 'a comedy with a catch in it'. The comedy was awful and the catch was on the audience.

Mr John Gielgud is a very good actor; but not in farce; as the young doctor who is in love with Vera he was hopelessly lost, and no wonder.
    J.G. BERGEL *EVENING NEWS*

FORTUNATO – 1928

*John Gielgud as Alberto, Fewlass Llewellyn as Don Victorio and
Catharina Ferraz as a dressmaker's assistant in Serafín and
Joaquín Alvarez Quintero's* Fortunato, *directed by James Whale
at the Royal Court Theatre.*

FORTUNATO, a tragi-farce, is the story of two beggars,
one professional, the other amateur. Gielgud played
the amateur who was more professional than the professional.

This picturesque study of poverty played in a double-
bill with the Quinteros' sentimental farce, *The Lady from
Alfáqueque.*

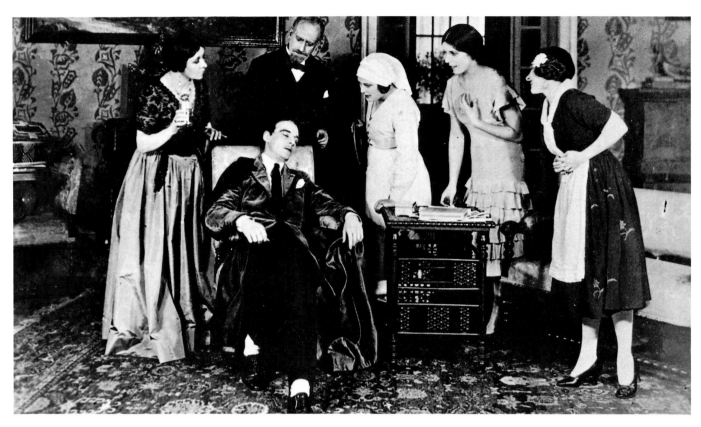

THE LADY FROM ALFÁQUEQUE – 1928

Gillian Scaife as Fernandita, Eric Stanley as Don Pascual, John Gielgud as Felipe Rivas, Margaret Webster as Paloma, Molly Rankin as Blanca and Ann Trevor as Rosita in Serafin and Joaquín Alvarez Quintero's The Lady from Alfáqueque, *directed by James Whale at the Royal Court Theatre.*

THE LADY is so charitable that everybody takes advantage of her. Felipe Rivas is no exception; but unlike all the others, he is no imposter, being exactly what he says he is – a real poet.

RED RUST – 1929

John Gielgud (in doorway) as Fédor, Harold Young (in white tunic) as Andrei and Margaret Swallow (far right) as Varvara in V.M. Kirchon and A.V. Ouspensky's Red Rust, *directed by Frank Vernon at the Little Theatre.*

RED RUST, a melodramatic murder story, was the first post-Russian Revolutionary drama to reach London. The production turned a pro-Bolshevik play into an anti-Bolshevik propaganda piece. Gielgud played an idealistic student.

THE CLUE OF THE NEW PIN – 1929

John Gielgud as Rex Trasmere, Kim Peacock as Tab Holland and Colin Kenny as Inspector Carver in Edgar Wallace's The Clue of the New Pin, *a silent film directed by Arthur Maude.*

GIELGUD played the murderer.

RICHARD II – 1929

John Gielgud as Richard in Shakespeare's Richard II, *directed by Harcourt Williams at the Old Vic Theatre.*

Asked by Harold Hobson, in 1961, which part he had most identified himself with, he replied instantly Richard II, adding with characteristic self-deprecation that Richard was 'a shallow young man, vain of his looks, with lovely things to say. I fancied myself no end in the part, but even that seemed to help my acting of it'.

A work of genuine distinction, not only in its grasp of character but in its control of language.
THE TIMES

ROMEO AND JULIET – 1929

Adele Dixon as Juliet and John Gielgud as Romeo in Shakespeare's Romeo and Juliet, *directed by Harcourt Williams at the Old Vic Theatre.*

Harcourt Williams, stop-watch in hand at rehearsals, was determined that *Romeo and Juliet* would be what Shakespeare said it was – a *two hours' traffic of our stage*. Such was the pace, on the first night, that audiences and critics complained they could not keep up.

The Terry voice is still lovely, however fast it speaks.
J.G. BERGEL EVENING NEWS

His delivery of the verse was various and delicate, his voice the fresh young voice of Romeo.
THE TIMES

1930s

John Geilgud in Hamlet *1934.*

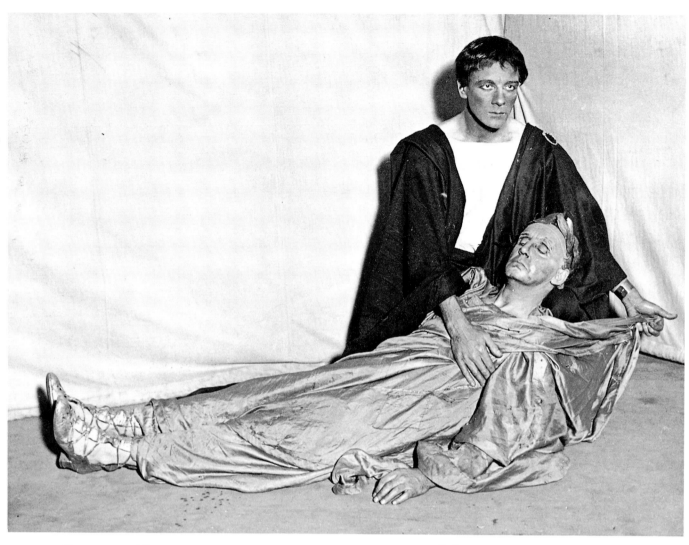

JULIUS CAESAR – 1930

John Gielgud as Mark Antony and Brember Wills as Julius Caesar in Shakespeare's Julius Caesar, *directed by Harcourt Williams at the Old Vic Theatre.*

MACBETH – 1930

John Gielgud as Macbeth in Shakespeare's Macbeth, *directed by Harcourt Williams at the Old Vic Theatre.*

The young actor, in my judgement, easily outdistanced all his predecessors, and revealed a promise which, when, as we all expect, it comes to complete fulfilment, must be what we have long waited for – an actor acknowledged national supremacy in the great Shakespearian roles.
ALAN PARSONS *DAILY MAIL*

BUT WHEN the play transferred to the Queen's Theatre, West End audiences stayed away.

Pit, upper circle and gallery are crowded at every performance. The more expensive parts of the house decline to be filled. It is a horrible thing to have to say, but I shall go on saying it: the rich have no taste in matters of the theatre, and those who have theatrical taste have no money. In other words, the serious theatre in this country is entirely supported by people who can hardly support themselves.
GEORGE WARRINGTON *COUNTRY LIFE*

HAMLET – 1930

Martita Hunt as Gertrude and John Gielgud as Hamlet in Shakespeare's Hamlet, *directed by Harcourt Williams at the Old Vic Theatre.*

AT TWENTY-SIX, Gielgud was the youngest Prince in living memory.

I have no hesitation whatsoever in saying that it is the high-water mark of English Shakespearian acting of our time.
JAMES AGATE *SUNDAY TIMES*

He is the most natural, the most sensitive and the most pathetic Hamlet I have seen.
E.A. BAUGHAN *NEWS CHRONICLE*

The performance puts him beyond the range of the arriving actors; he is in the first rank.
IVOR BROWN *OBSERVER*

THE IMPORTANCE OF BEING EARNEST – 1930

John Gielgud as John Worthing, Iris Baker as Gwendolen Fairfax, Heather Angel as Cecily Cardew and Anthony Ireland as Algernon Moncrieff in Oscar Wilde's The Importance of Being Earnest, *directed by Nigel Playfair at the Lyric Theatre, Hammersmith.*

NIGEL PLAYFAIR's production was a stylised black-and-white affair in the Aubrey Beardsley manner. Gielgud, speaking fast, lightly and with exquisite precision, had an instinctive feeling for the period and Wilde's wit.

He confirms the impression that deepens with every performance that he is a young man with a very great future.
MONICA EWER *DAILY HERALD*

Mr Gielgud is totally unfitted for the part, not because he is a tragic actor, but because he is a serious one.
JAMES AGATE *SUNDAY TIMES*

GIELGUD would return to *The Importance of Being Earnest* with even greater success in 1939; but James Agate never changed his mind.

THE TEMPEST – 1930

John Gielgud as Prospero and Leslie French as Ariel in Shakespeare's The Tempest, *directed by Harcourt Williams at the Old Vic Theatre.*

Looking like a Doge just stepped from the canvas of an Italian master, Mr John Gielgud made a stately Prospero of uncommon distinction.

THE TIMES

ANTONY AND CLEOPATRA – 1930

Dorothy Green as Cleopatra and John Gielgud as Antony in Shakespeare's Antony and Cleopatra, *directed by Harcourt Williams at the Old Vic Theatre.*

HARCOURT WILLIAMS's production was staged with Renaissance classical scenery and dressed in the style of Veronese.

Gielgud's Antony (a grizzle-bearded Elizabethan adventurer) was confident with the rhetoric and extravagant romanticism, but inevitably he lacked the maturity and animal sensuality the role should have.

TWELFTH NIGHT – 1931

John Gielgud as Malvolio, Dorothy Green as Viola, Valentine Dyall as a priest, George Howe as Sir Andrew Aguecheek and Ralph Richardson as Sir Toby Belch in Shakespeare's Twelfth Night, *directed by Harcourt Williams at Sadler's Wells Theatre and the Old Vic Theatre. Harcourt Williams can be seen standing at the far right of the stage.*

SADLER'S WELLS THEATRE re-opened, under Lilian Baylis's management, on twelfth night, with this production. The occasion was better than the performance.

ARMS AND THE MAN – 1931

John Gielgud as Sergius Saranoff in Bernard Shaw's Arms and the Man, *directed by Harcourt Williams at the Old Vic Theatre.*

SERGIUS, an amateur soldier, enamoured by the idea of the Heroic Ideal (a concept he picked up at the opera house) leads a lunatic yet highly successful cavalry charge against an enemy armed with machine-guns. He becomes the hero of the hour and the darling of the regiment. The man is a buffoon and Gielgud played him very broadly.

KING LEAR – 1931

John Gielgud as Lear in Shakespeare's King Lear, *directed by Harcourt Williams at the Old Vic Theatre.*

WHAT HAD IMPRESSED Gielgud in his study of the part was the sheer physical strength of Lear and he based his make-up on a seventeenth-century portrait of Anger.

Though he did not conquer Everest – the storm dominated him, rather than he it – he failed in a manner which made it realistic to hope that one day he would succeed.

Mr Gielgud rode his private whirlwind down the road to madness with a shade too much declamation. The imminence of collapse never terrified; it had the deliberate threat of distant gunfire rather than the unpredictable menace of a volcano.

PETER FLEMING *SPECTATOR*

Lear shrieks out to be acted and if I may say so in all modesty I am not terrified by the part. What does terrify me is the idea of going back to modern plays and appearing as an ordinary young man after playing in the Shakespearian tragedies. . . . There are scenes in which I knew I was bound to fail. I haven't the voice; there is no getting away from the fact. I realise the storm scenes fail, and it is my fault. Lear has to be the storm. But I am pleased I have tackled the part and extremely grateful that I have been taken seriously. I hope to have another shot at Hamlet and Richard in two or five years time, and Lear and Macbeth in twenty. The part I should like to play in Lear now is the fool.

JOHN GIELGUD

LEAR would be a role to which he would return at ten-yearly intervals.

THE GOOD COMPANIONS – 1931

*Adele Dixon as Susie Dean, John Gielgud as Inigo Jollifant,
Deering Wells as Fauntley and Lawrence Baskomb as Morton
Mitcham in J.B. Priestley and Edward Knoblock's adaptation of
J.B. Priestley's* The Good Companions, *directed by Julian Wylie
at His Majesty's Theatre.*

THE ONLY PEOPLE who would seem not to have read
Priestley's best-selling novel were the critics, who
found the stage adaptation a bit too picaresque for their
liking. They were also disconcerted by a first-night
audience who greeted all the characters as if they were
personal friends.

Gielgud was cast as the young preparatory schoolmaster who turns professional pianist and composer to a
pierrot troupe. There were those who felt, after his
brilliant seasons at the Old Vic, that he should be doing
something more taxing and less dinky-do than playing
the romantic juvenile lead in a West End show.

MUSICAL CHAIRS – 1931

Margaret Webster as Mary Preston and John Gielgud as Joseph Schindler in Ronald Mackenzie's Musical Chairs, *directed by Theodore Komisarjevsky at the Arts Theatre. The production transferred to the Criterion Theatre in 1932.*

JAMES AGATE described *Musical Chairs* as 'the best first play written by an English playwright during the last forty years'.

The play, a tragi-comedy in the Russian manner, was set among the oil fields in Galicia, Poland, and Gielgud played a cynical and consumptive pianist whose German fiancée had been killed during the war. She had died during the bombing of Düsseldorf, in an air-raid in which he had participated. His piano-playing was praised as highly as his acting.

Mr Gielgud's acting was a wonderfully convincing mixture of nervous exasperation and real emotion.
DESMOND MACCARTHY *NEW STATESMAN AND NATION*

It is a great performance – delicate, sensitive, discreet, restrained.
ALAN PARSONS *DAILY MAIL*

INSULT – 1932

John Gielgud as Henri Dubois and Sam Livesey as Major Dubois in the film version of Jan Fabricus's play Insult, *directed by Harry Lachman.*

INSULT, a long-forgotten colonial drama set in Africa, was Gielgud's first talkie.

THE GOOD COMPANIONS – 1932

John Gielgud as Inigo Jollifant and, far left, Finlay Currie as Monte Mortimer in the film version of J.B. Priestley's The Good Companions, *directed by Victor Saville.*

IN THE SAME WAY that Edward Chapman, playing Oakroyd, had dominated the play, so now Edmund Gwenn, in the same role, dominated the film.

Gielgud spent much of his time, with his back to the camera, sitting at a piano in a pierrot costume, accompanying Jessie Matthews. He flirted, bickered, sang, and, at one point, was seen coyly conducting a West End show. Most amazing of all was the sight of him acting as 'feed' to the music hall comedian Max Miller. His best scene, as it had been in the theatre, was in the music publisher's office.

It suggests a long screen career for John Gielgud, who plays Jollifant.
C.A. LEJEUNE *OBSERVER*

Many years ago King George and Queen Mary came to a gala performance of Richard of Bordeaux *in aid of the King George Pension Fund. John and I were to be presented in the interval. In some agitation John came to my dressing-room to ask whether I thought he should wear his crown. I said I thought he should – and he did and has worn it ever since. 'The observed of all observers' and greatly loved.*

GWEN FFRANGCON-DAVIES

RICHARD OF BORDEAUX – 1933

John Gielgud as Richard in Gordon Daviot's Richard of Bordeaux, *directed by John Gielgud at the New Theatre.*

Mr Gielgud's performance is a marvellous combination of vacillation, nobility, and embittered disillusion, finely restrained even in his most passionate outbursts. This is genuinely great acting which has the power to thrill in its intensity.

HAROLD CONWAY *DAILY MAIL*

In this play he takes his place among the first of his actors – his presence, his intellectual grasp, his penetrating strength, and his diction give that power and authenticity that belong to supreme acting.

J.T. GREIN *SKETCH*

As acting, nothing to equal it can be seen today on the English stage.

SYDNEY W. CARROLL *DAILY TELEGRAPH*

In my opinion, he is now the first of English actors. It is far from being an age of great acting, but the range of his emotional scope, and the intelligence with which he conceives parts, put him right at the top of the profession. He combines the histrionic temperament with interpretative intelligence; that is rare.

DESMOND MACCARTHY *NEW STATESMAN AND NATION*

THE MAITLANDS – 1934

Sophie Stewart as Joan Clareville and John Gielgud as Roger Maitland in Ronald Mackenzie's The Maitlands, *directed by Theodore Komisarjevsky at the Wyndham's Theatre.*

THE MAITLANDS, produced posthumously, (the author having been killed in a car accident in France), did not repeat the success of *Musical Chairs*. Gielgud felt that the director and actors had not exploited Mackenzie's theatrical effects to the full. He himself was not particularly well cast as the neurotic, second-rate schoolteacher whose wife has left him; and he wasn't convincing in a scene where he had to get drunk.

HAMLET – 1934

Frank Vosper as Claudius, Alec Guinness as Osric, Glen Byam Shaw as Laertes, John Gielgud as Hamlet, Jack Hawkins as Horatio and Laura Cowie as Gertrude in Shakespeare's Hamlet, *directed by John Gielgud at the New Theatre.*

IT WAS DIFFICULT, for many people, to believe that there had ever been or ever would be a better Hamlet. Gielgud had re-created the role for a post-war audience in a post-war way.

In every syllable that he speaks, there is evidence of an understanding mind at work so that the lines come fresh to the minds of the audience as if the part had never been acted before.
W.A. DARLINGTON *DAILY TELEGRAPH*

It is the glory of the stage today.
M. WILLSON DISHER *DAILY MAIL*

Altogether the best production of Hamlet *which I have ever seen or am ever likely to see.*
RAYMOND MORTIMER *NEW STATESMAN AND NATION*

As acting, nothing to equal it can be seen today on the English stage.
SYDNEY W. CARROLL *DAILY TELEGRAPH*

If I see a better performance of the play than this before I die, it will be a miracle.
CHARLES MORGAN *NEW STATESMAN AND NATION*

He rather gave me the impression of a moody modern youth who needed spanking.
W. JESSE COLLINGS *DAILY SKETCH*

NOAH – 1935

John Gielgud as Noah in André Obey's Noah, *directed by Michel Saint-Denis at the New Theatre.*

Mr Gielgud's Noah, with his six-hundred-year-old body so swadled and hirsute as to make summer nights seem a dreadful thought, is a prodigious mixture of Lear, Job, Tolstoy, and the Old Man of the Sea plagued with a Load of Mischief.

IVOR BROWN *OBSERVER*

ANDRÉ OBEY's biblical pantomime for adult children had already been seen in London, in French, four years earlier, in an enchanting production by the *Compagnie des Quinze*. The American translation did not begin to do justice to its quaint naivety and poetry.

The play opened during a heat-wave.

ROMEO AND JULIET – 1935

Laurence Olivier as Romeo, Glen Byam Shaw as Benvolio, John Gielgud as Mercutio and Geoffrey Toone as Tybalt in Shakespeare's Romeo and Juliet, directed by John Gielgud at the New Theatre.

John Gielgud as Mercutio, Laurence Olivier as Romeo, Glen Byam Shaw as Benvolio, Frederick Lloyd as Capulet, Peggy Ashcroft as Juliet and Edith Evans as the Nurse in Romeo and Juliet.

THIS was the famous production in which Gielgud and Olivier, in their first and last appearance together in a play, alternated the lead-role and Mercutio.

Mr Gielgud's Mercutio is a brilliant performance, executed with finish and power. No more gallant death has ever been died by this most gallant gentleman.
W.A. DARLINGTON *DAILY TELEGRAPH*

He lived like a rake and died like a gentleman – all too soon for my liking.
STEPHEN WILLIAMS *EVENING STANDARD*

Mr Gielgud's own vital, courageous Mercutio is an outstanding performance – less bitter than most; his Queen Mab speech was exquisite and his death scene a wonderful suggestion of disillusioned chivalry.
P.L. MANNOCK *DAILY HERALD*

I have seen better Mercutios than John Gielgud. His death scene is disappointing. Too much charm and not enough bitter physical pain. The 'Plague on both your houses' was surely no playful jest.
HERBERT FARJEON *SUNDAY PICTORIAL*

ROMEO AND JULIET – 1935

John Gielgud as Romeo in Shakespeare's Romeo and Juliet, *directed by John Gielgud at the New Theatre.*

It seems to me incontestable that Mr Gielgud is the better Romeo. For Romeo was a poet.
J.G. BERGEL *EVENING NEWS*

Mr Gielgud seems to me almost the perfect Romeo.
BERNARD BUCKHAM *DAILY MIRROR*

As Romeo Mr Olivier was about twenty times as much in love with Juliet as Mr Gielgud is. But Mr Gielgud speaks most of the poetry far better than Mr Olivier.
HERBERT FARJEON *SUNDAY PICTORIAL*

Mr Olivier's Romeo showed himself very much in love but rather butchered the poetry, whereas Mr Gielgud curves the verse so exquisitely that you would say the shop he kept was a bonne-boucherie. (If an Englishman may not pun in French in what language may he pun?) Yet is this Romeo ever really in love with anybody except himself?
JAMES AGATE *SUNDAY TIMES*

Not the least of the things that I love Johnnie Gielgud for is his extraordinary gift for dropping bricks. There remains forever, however, my devotion to him which has lasted since his generosity in asking me to play Romeo and Mercutio alternately with him way back in 1935. We have met with the greatest frequence we have been allowed over the years, and I personally wish it could have been more often. I remember coming off stage in the middle of one matinee as Mercutio and saying 'It's a terrible lot out there — I can't get a smile out of the bastards', and he said without thinking as usual, 'Of course not, there are no cheap parts in front.' I have ever loved him dearly and I always shall.

LAURENCE OLIVIER

John Gielgud as Romeo and Peggy Ashcroft as Juliet in Shakespeare's Romeo and Juliet.

THE SEAGULL – 1936

*Edith Evans as Irina Arcadina and John Gielgud as Boris
Trigorin in Anton Chekhov's* The Seagull, *directed by
Theodore Komisarjevsky at the New Theatre.*

THE SEAGULL was the first full-scale production of a
Chekhov play in the West End and was, by common
consent, the highwater mark of Komisarjevsky's achievement, famous for its poetic beauty and fine ensemble
playing.

Audiences, who arrived at the theatre expecting
Trigorin to be a down-at-heel, cigar-smoking genius, in
check-trousers, were surprised to find an elegant, essentially second-rate writer who looked like a gigolo and
smoked cigarettes. It was the dilettante shallowness and
vanity of the man which Gielgud so sensitively satirised.

HAMLET – 1936

*John Gielgud as Hamlet and Judith Anderson as Gertrude in
Shakespeare's* Hamlet, *directed by Guthrie McClintic at the
Empire Theatre, New York. The production transferred to the
St James's Theatre.*

GIELGUD'S Hamlet was the most eagerly awaited
Hamlet since John Barrymore's. The critics
admired his performance for its spontaneity and clarity,
its passion and conviction, its vitality and magnetism, its
rapid cinematic tempo, its cerebral incisiveness, above all
for its youth, grace and eloquence.

*Let it be recorded here that he is one of the greatest living
Hamlets of our time.*
EDGAR PRICE *CITIZEN*

*There have been many notable performances of Hamlet,
even in the limited theatre of our time, but none of them
has achieved so completely as this, the triumph of
Shakespeare's poetry.*
EDITH J.R. ISSACS *THEATRE ARTS MONTHLY*

*It is soaring magic and its like has not been in our town for
years.*
WHITNEY BOLTON *NEW YORK TELEGRAPH*

*John Gielgud is an extraordinary actor, a vivid, violent
theatrical Hamlet, endowed with the ability to raise an
audience to fever pitch without ever once sacrificing the
beauty of the poet's words. . . . His greatest asset is his voice,
which is unlike any I have ever heard. It is like a musical
instrument on which he plays at will, lightly and expertly.*
ELLIOT NORTON *POST, BOSTON*

THE production was a smash-hit, playing 132 times in
New York alone, breaking the Barrymore record of 101
performances.

THE SECRET AGENT – 1936

John Gielgud as Ashenden, Madeleine Carroll as Elsa and Peter Lorre as the Mexican in The Secret Agent, *a film directed by Alfred Hitchcock.*

THE SECRET AGENT was a bit of a disappointment after the excitement of *The Thirty-Nine Steps* and *The Man Who Knew Too Much*, though there were some characteristic Hitchcockian touches during the events leading to the murder where the tension was created almost entirely by a fretting dog, back at the hotel, far away from the scene of the crime.

Gielgud was cast as a novelist-turned-spy who kills the wrong man, an innocent tourist. He and Madeleine Carroll played their love scenes in the familiar 1930s Noel Coward clipped vowel 'Don't-cry-have-a-cigarette' manner.

Peter Lorre, professional scene-stealer, hogged the screen as the unlikeliest and campest womaniser who was also the chief assassin.

From our point of view, of course, he is quite inexperienced. He's a beginner. His stage experience is no use to him here. I've had to make him rub out everything and start blank. I have to rely purely on his intelligence to get him to do what is wanted.

ALFRED HITCHCOCK

Mr Gielgud is without question the leading actor of our age, and it is a curious comment on the stage and the screen that whereas in any stage scene he is always the dominant person, in the picture one had to look to find him. Not that his part offered him much help.

MIDLAND COUNTIES EXPRESS

As Ashenden, John Gielgud walks through his part and since the character he is enacting is not endowed with a superabundance of intelligence, he fails to make it register very forcibly.

PICTUREGOER

HE WAS BORN GAY – 1937

Sydney Fairbrother as Lady Atkyns, John Gielgud as Mason, Frank Pettingell as Mr Leroy, Betty Jardine as Prissy Dell, Glen Byam Shaw as Lewis Dell, Elliot Mason as Mrs Georgina Dell and Carol Goodner as Sophy Rafferty in Emlyn Williams's He Was Born Gay, *directed by John Gielgud in conjunction with the author at the Queen's Theatre.*

Gielgud was cast as the son of Marie Antoinette, the lost Dauphin of the Temple, Louis XVII, now grown-up, disguised as a music master, and in England.

Emlyn Williams's improbable romantic fiction, which ended in Louis's suicide, was not helped by the addition of two farcical claimants to the throne.

Gielgud's best moments came in the second act when he remembered his childhood at Versailles, the horrors of the French Revolution and the day his father was guillotined.

RICHARD II – 1937

Glen Byam Shaw as Thomas Mowbray, Leon Quartermaine as John of Gaunt, Peggy Ashcroft as Queen, John Gielgud as Richard and Michael Redgrave as Henry Bolingbroke in Shakespeare's Richard II, *directed by John Gielgud at the Queen's Theatre.*

He has never shown a finer sensibility to beauty, his voice has never before displayed so wide a range, and his major fault – a tendency to an hysterical sharpness in that voice's highest register as distinct from its loudest – has not in any performance since his Old Vic days been less in evidence.
ALAN DENT *MANCHESTER GUARDIAN*

It is more simple, more flexible, more mature; he has shed almost all his mannerisms (and those which he retains one need not grudge him), and he has freed himself of a tendency to rhetoric.
DEREK VERSCHOYLE *SPECTATOR*

THE SCHOOL FOR SCANDAL – 1937

John Gielgud as Joseph Surface in Richard Brinsley Sheridan's The School for Scandal, *directed by Tyrone Guthrie at the Queen's Theatre.*

GIELGUD'S smooth-tongued hypocrite was the subtlest and most plausible of villains: his witty, stylish, highly polished performance raised dissembling to a fine art.

Tyrone Guthrie's production was thought to be something of a scandal. There was so much bowing, skipping and pirouetting that many critics felt they were assisting at a performance of *Les Ballets Russes* rather than Sheridan.

What he brought out admirably was that Joseph is not only a hypocrite but a completely self-conscious hypocrite (hardly ever to be found in real life) who delights like an artist in his own hypocrisy. That is the main point of the part and he hit it perfectly.
DESMOND MACCARTHY *NEW STATESMAN AND NATION*

THREE SISTERS – 1938

Peggy Ashcroft as Irina, John Gielgud as Vershinin, Carol Goodner as Masha and Gwen Ffrangcon-Davies as Olga in Anton Chekhov's Three Sisters, *directed by Michel Saint-Denis at the Queen's Theatre.*

Michel Saint-Denis's production, universally praised for its meticulous detail, poignant beauty and fine ensemble work of a distinguished cast, was one of the great Chekhovian productions of the 1930s.

Gielgud was made-up to resemble the contemporary portraits of Stanislavski's Vershinin.

What could be more convincing and satisfying than the controlled impetuosity, the fervent sincerity yet comicality of John Gielgud's Vershinin.
SYDNEY W. CARROLL *DAILY TELEGRAPH*

Mr Gielgud's Colonel Alexander Ignatyevitch Vershinin is one of his best performances. A fault he has, of underacting, is not apparent here. He draws Vershinin's feeble character with exquisite skill, clearly showing us the man's small egotism, the vanity of his futile speculations and knowledge, his ineffable priggishness, his essential infelicity.
ST JOHN ERVINE *OBSERVER*

THE MERCHANT OF VENICE –
1938

John Gielgud as Shylock in Shakespeare's The Merchant of
Venice, *directed by John Gielgud and Glen Byam Shaw at the
Queen's Theatre.*

G IELGUD's unselfish acknowledgement that *The Merchant of Venice* is not just about Shylock benefited
the play as a whole and Peggy Ashcroft's Portia in
particular; but inevitably it did disappoint those who had
come to see *Gielgud's* Shylock, and even more so when
he failed to give them the Henry Irving-like histrionics
they wanted and provided something altogether more
subdued, grubbier, uglier, meaner – a Jew, in short, who
made no appeal for pity and inspired none.

    There were those, Laurence Olivier among them,
who rated Shylock among his best work, but they were in
the minority. Gielgud himself thought he had failed.

*His Shylock reaches for no height, and touches none.
Shylock is a great actor's part, a thing to colour and design.
Mr Gielgud photographs it.*
LIONEL HALE *NEWS CHRONICLE*

*One could find many things to say in favour of this
performance. One could praise its measure, restraint,
intellectuality, if one thought that these qualities ought to
be in Shylock. But suppose one holds that what the part
calls for is hatred and demonic fury? Suppose one sees
Shylock as storm-centre, malignant and terrible, ready to
shatter the inconsiderable world about him? What, then,
holding this view, is one to say of a Shylock who is merely
a wet blanket at a party?*
JAMES AGATE *SUNDAY TIMES*

*Mr John Gielgud's Shylock is the most human and credible
I have ever seen.*
STEPHEN WILLIAMS *EVENING STANDARD*

DEAR OCTOPUS – 1938

John Gielgud as Nicholas Randolph, Una Venning as Edna Randolph, John Justin as Hugh Randolph, Jean Ormonde as Laurel Randolph, Angela Baddeley as Fenny, Nan Munro as Hilda Randolph, Kate Cutler as Belle Schlesinger, Leon Quartermaine as Charles Randolph, Madge Compton as Margery Harvey, Pat Sylvester as Bill, Sylvia Hammond as Flouncey, Muriel Pavlow as Scrap, Valerie Taylor as Cynthia Randolph, Felix Irwin as Kenneth Harvey and Marie Tempest as Dora Randolph in Dodie Smith's Dear Octopus, directed by Glen Byam Shaw at the Queen's Theatre.

THREE generations get together to celebrate a couple's golden wedding anniversary. Gielgud, as the eldest son, is seen here proposing the Grand Toast: 'To the family – that dear octopus whose tentacles we never quite escape, nor, in our inmost hearts, ever quite wish to.'

Dodie Smith's homily about accepting middle and old age, was efficiently tailored to West End taste: a charming, cosy kind of play, all sentiment, no bite and no depth.

HAMLET – 1939

John Gielgud as Hamlet and Fay Compton as Ophelia in Shakespeare's Hamlet, *directed by John Gielgud at Kronborg Castle, Elsinore.*

The performance will give Elsinore a world-reputation equal to that of Oberammergau.
BERLINGSKE TIDENDE

THE IMPORTANCE OF BEING EARNEST – 1939

Gwen Ffrangcon-Davies as Gwendolen Fairfax, John Gielgud as John Worthing and Edith Evans as Lady Bracknell in Oscar Wilde's The Importance of Being Earnest, *directed by John Gielgud at the Globe Theatre.*

THE IMPORTANCE OF BEING EARNEST – 1939

John Gielgud as John Worthing, Gwen Ffrangcon-Davies as Gwendolen Fairfax, Peggy Ashcroft as Cecily Cardew and Jack Hawkins as Algernon Moncrieff in Oscar Wilde's The Importance of Being Earnest, *directed by John Gielgud at the Globe Theatre.*

Gielgud's production, hailed as the most subtle treatment of the play anybody could remember, was immortalised by Edith Evans's definitive Lady Bracknell, whose amazement, on learning that Mr Worthing had been born in *a handbag*, is probably still the most quoted and imitated phrase in British theatre.

Wilde's brilliant epigrammatic dialogue was delivered by a cast who had a perfect understanding of the author's philosophy: namely that we should treat all the trivial things of life seriously and all the serious things of life with sincere and studied triviality.

Mr Gielgud's John Worthing is full of rare comedy; he passes from mourning to muffins with a measured dignity that is never over-done and he adds subtlety and freshness to the value of familiar lines.

IVOR BROWN *OBSERVER*

John Gielgud's light, clear, civilised performance unfalteringly holds the balance of the comedy true. It is a masterpiece of artificial acting.

A.V. COOKMAN *BYSTANDER*

Mr John Gielgud, as John Worthing, is nothing short of brilliant. He has, so to speak, disappeared into the period, so right is he and so unforced is his comedy.

W.A. DARLINGTON *DAILY TELEGRAPH*

1940s

John Gielgud as Valentine in Love for Love *1944.*

KING LEAR – 1940

John Gielgud as Lear in Shakespeare's King Lear, *directed by Lewis Casson and Harley Granville-Barker at the Old Vic Theatre.*

Lear should be an oak. You'll never be that, but we might make something of you as an ash.
HARLEY GRANVILLE-BARKER

The Olympian grandeur, the frets, the rages, the madness lit with flashes of savage irony and broken in upon by spiritual illumination – all these phases of the part he succeeded in treating as though they were a spontaneous product of the mind, but the simplicities of the end he surrounded with a stillness of beauty which is rarely achieved on the stage.
THE TIMES

The first act is nothing short of superb and in the last three there is a depth of pathos which we have never had much reason to suspect before. This acting gives us much of the terror of the play, and still more the pity of it. It is only in the easiest and least important scenes, occurring early, that we faintly detect the young actor in his thirties behind that old and most authoritative beard.
ALAN DENT MANCHESTER GUARDIAN

THE TEMPEST – 1940

John Gielgud as Prospero in Shakespeare's The Tempest, *directed by George Devine and Marius Goring at the Old Vic Theatre.*

Mr Gielgud's Prospero, very far from the usual mixture of Father Christmas, a Colonial Bishop, and the President of the Magicians' Union, is a clear, arresting picture of a virile Renaissance notable (no dotard) who has 'a daily beauty in his life' as well as magic powers.
IVOR BROWN OBSERVER

DEAR BRUTUS – 1941

Margaret Rawlings as Mrs Dearth and John Gielgud as Mr Dearth in J.M. Barrie's Dear Brutus, *directed by John Gielgud at the Globe Theatre.*

A GROUP of people, on midsummer's eve, are given a second chance, an opportunity to find out what would have happened if they had not taken that wrong turning all those years ago.

The critics and Gielgud himself (who had attended the first night of the original production) did not feel he was as good as George du Maurier who had created the role of the painter who meets the child he had always wanted but never had – a bit of whimsy a 1917 audience had found easier to take.

To the notorious and unremunerative part of Dearth, Mr Gielgud has devoted his immense talent – nobody could make it more palatable.
GRAHAM GREENE *SPECTATOR*

THE PRIME MINISTER – 1941

Diana Wynyard as Anne Wyndham Lewis and John Gielgud as Benjamin Disraeli in The Prime Minister, *a film directed by Thorold Dickenson.*

THE PRIME MINISTER (known in the trade as *Sixty Laborious Years*) was biography and history turned into romantic fiction and war-time propaganda.

Gielgud's young Dizzy was a very self-conscious and stagey Regency dandy; while his elder statesman looked all set to act Shylock and could have fitted, with ease, into Jonathan Miller's Victorian production of *The Merchant of Venice* at the National Theatre thirty years later.

In the second part of the film, which drew parallels between the political situation in 1874 and 1941, he spent most of his time making long and boring speeches justifying the Second World War.

The final scene, played for some very cheap laughs, in which Disraeli saves England by getting Bismarck drunk, was a farcical coda, which would have been more appropriate in Charlie Chaplin's *The Great Dictator*.

MACBETH – 1942

John Gielgud as Macbeth and Gwen Ffrangcon-Davies as Lady Macbeth in Shakespeare's Macbeth, *directed by John Gielgud at the Piccadilly Theatre.*

Mr Gielgud seems to me to have never, in the whole of his career, played with more finesse, subtlety, poetry, fire, clearness and authority than he did on the first night at the Piccadilly.

ALAN DENT *TIME AND TIDE*

The performance is truly exciting when Macbeth, between one murder and another, falls prey to his wildly superstitious nature and paints imaginary horror in words that seem to have been dipped in the witches' cauldron. Then Mr Gielgud's voice and his power to express fine shades of differing emotions came into their own and the stage is thrillingly alive.

THE TIMES

Moreover, Mr Gielgud, whose voice is a magnificent organ, treats it like a Wurlitzer, pulling out different stops in every other word. These ornamentations vulgarise the harmony just as the pauses and syncopations wreck the melody. There is hardly a line in which the rise and fall of the verse are preserved, and never a passage in which an attempt is not made to improve upon Shakespeare's incomparably varied versifications. Mr Gielgud can, we know, speak blank verse very finely; but often in this production one seemed to be listening to a cruel skit in a revue upon his mannerisms.

ROGER MARVELL *NEW STATESMAN AND NATION*

THE DOCTOR'S DILEMMA – 1943

Vivien Leigh as Jennifer Dubedat and John Gielgud as Louis Dubedat in George Bernard Shaw's The Doctor's Dilemma, *directed by Irene Hentschel at the Theatre Royal, Haymarket.*

GIELGUD took over the role, at twenty-four hours notice, when Peter Glenville *and* his understudy were taken ill. He played Dubedat for a week.

LOVE FOR LOVE – 1944

Cecil Trouncer as Sir Sampson Legend, Leon Quartermaine as Scandal, J.D. Williams as Buckram, John Gielgud as Valentine and Max Adrian as Jeremy in William Congreve's Love for Love, directed by John Gielgud at the Theatre Royal, Haymarket.

Love for Love is a much better play than *The Way of the World* and it is always surprising that it is not revived more often.

The high spot of Gielgud's performance was Valentine's feigned madness (a bravura parody of his own Hamlet's antic disposition) where he looked, for all the world, as if he had, however unwittingly, stepped right out of Robert Smirk's famous eighteenth-century painting. The scene gained enormously from the unexpected seriousness with which he spoke his mind and heart to Angelica in the middle of all the farcical goings-on.

John Gielgud's brilliant production, with a cast unequalled in London, easily sails past the censor. It is at once the naughtiest and most civilised play in town.
ERNEST BETTS *DAILY EXPRESS*

Playgoers who fail to see Love for Love *will have missed something quite outstanding.*
JAMES REDFERN *SPECTATOR*

THE CIRCLE – 1944

John Gielgud as Arnold Champion-Cheney, MP and Rosalie Crutchley as Elizabeth in W. Somerset Maugham's The Circle, *directed by William Armstrong at the Theatre Royal, Haymarket.*

THE CIRCLE is a civilised, witty entertainment; a cruel comedy of 1920s manners in Somerset Maugham's best cynical vein.

This revival, by putting the play back to the more glamorous Edwardian era and by casting the vivacious Yvonne Arnaud as the pathetic Lady Kitty, inevitably cut down on the cruelty and merely emphasised Maugham's epigrammatic affinity with Wilde.

Gielgud, as the self-centred, icily cold, priggish husband, was very funny: 'You can't expect a man to go on making love to his wife after three years. I'm very busy. After all a man marries to have a home, but also because he doesn't want to bother with sex and all that sort of thing.'

What an actor this is! He can poise a line like a foil and put it home with the most delicate turn of the wrist. He matches Mr Maugham's irony – and even the Theatre Royal, Haymarket, in grace.
LIONEL HALE *MANCHESTER GUARDIAN*

HAMLET – 1944

John Gielgud as Hamlet in Shakespeare's Hamlet, *directed by George Rylands at the Theatre Royal, Haymarket.*

In short, I hold that this is, and is likely to remain the best Hamlet of our time, and that is why I urge Mr Gielgud to stick to the mantle of tragedy and leave lesser garments to others.

JAMES AGATE *SUNDAY TIMES*

He sinks the actor in the part, the part more deeply in the play than of old, and his technique does not vaunt its virtuosity. The fruit of study and practice is plainly manifest.

HORACE HORSNELL *TATLER AND BYSTANDER*

Gielgud's Hamlet is one of the great performances of our time and perhaps of all time.

W.A. DARLINGTON *NEW YORK TIMES*

A MIDSUMMER NIGHT'S DREAM – 1945

Max Adrian as Puck, Peggy Ashcroft as Titania and John Gielgud as Oberon in Shakespeare's A Midsummer Night's Dream, *directed by Nevill Coghill at the Theatre Royal, Haymarket.*

Most critics were disappointed that Mendelssohn's music had been dropped and that there was no ballet for the fairies. Few cared either for the costumes, Gielgud's appearance, the Inigo Jones masque element or for the mature young lovers (this being wartime all available Lysanders and Demetriuses had been called up).

Gielgud, with his greenish face, looked so grim and sinister, that he was likened to Julius Caesar's ghost, Hamlet's father, the Demon King, a misfit and a Roman centurion. He changed his make-up after the first night for something less autumnal and more midsummery.

The little duet, specially choreographed for Oberon and Titania by Frederick Ashton, was not greatly appreciated.

The formulism of fairyland was further emphasised when Mr Gielgud and Miss Ashcroft did a ballroom dance. One, two, three, twirl; one, two three, twirl. Just as I hoped they were going to do a rumba, it degenerated into a minuet, and then with a smile and a kingly gesture Mr Gielgud dismissed the lady.

BEVERLEY BAXTER *EVENING NEWS*

The theatrical atrocities, in Webster's dark chamber of horrors, as violent as in any Chicago gangster film, paled into insignificance when compared to the actual atrocities committed by the Nazis in concentration camps and which could be seen in 1945, for the first time, in newsreels in every cinema up and down the country.

Gielgud's Ferdinand was a performance of dazzling virtuosity, tense and high-pitched. Every young actor should see it, and having seen it go home and weep in sheer desperation.
BEVERLEY NICHOLS *SUNDAY CHRONICLE*

CRIME AND PUNISHMENT – 1946

John Gielgud as Raskolnikoff in Rodney Ackland's dramatisation of Fyodor Dostoyevsky's Crime and Punishment, *directed by Anthony Quayle at the New Theatre. The production transferred to the Globe Theatre.*

WHILE there were those who ranked Raskolnikoff among Gielgud's finest work – James Agate thought it was his best performance since Hamlet – there were others, however, including Peter Ustinov (who was playing Petrovitch, the police chief) who found him far too neurotic and wondered why the police chief didn't arrest him immediately.

If the first act performance of Mr Gielgud's is not great acting, I never saw it.
LIONEL HALE *DAILY MAIL*

Gielgud's performance as the murderer is an astonishing feat, rising to moments of sheer epileptic frenzy.
ERNEST BETTS *DAILY EXPRESS*

Mr Gielgud's suggestion of storm within and foreboding calm without is a cunning acting combination of passion and pease.
T.C. KEOWN *BIRMINGHAM POST*

Perhaps Mr Gielgud acted him too much on the same note, the quiet I-must-be-calm voice followed too quickly, too often, and too regularly by the nervous staccato outbreak. One longed for a minute of quietness, while one marvelled at the ability to keep at strain.
STEPHEN POTTER *NEW STATESMAN*

THE DUCHESS OF MALFI – 1945

John Gielgud as Ferdinand and Cecil Trouncer as Bosola in John Webster's The Duchess of Malfi, *directed by George Rylands at the Theatre Royal, Haymarket.*

FOR THOSE members of the audience who were wondering why the two brothers – the kinky cardinal and the paranoid Ferdinand – should want to torture the Duchess, their sister, Gielgud offered a Freudian interpretation: he objected to his sister's marriage because he wanted to marry her himself.

CRIME AND PUNISHMENT – 1947

John Gielgud as Raskolnikoff and Vladimir Sokoloff as Petrovitch in Rodney Ackland's dramatisation of Fyodor Dostoyevsky's Crime and Punishment, directed by Theodore Komisarjevsky at the National Theatre, New York.

As the intellectual murderer John Gielgud gives the most brilliant of his New York performances.
BROOKS ATKINSON *NEW YORK TIMES*

John Gielgud, on the far left of the picture, as Raskolnikoff, Dolly Haas, in the centre kneeling, as Sonia and Lillian Gish, standing next to her, as Katerina in Crime and Punishment.

MEDEA – 1947

*John Gielgud as Jason and Judith Anderson as Medea in
Euripides' Medea, directed by John Gielgud at the
National Theatre, New York.*

Medea is one of the world's great murder stories with a splendid twist when it is discovered the murder was totally unnecessary.

Judith Anderson scored an enormous critical success, but Gielgud, in a secondary role he had not wanted to play in the first place, was found to be colourless and lacking in power.

Gielgud's Jason is perhaps critically sound but such is the occasional eccentricity of the stage, it does not come off theatrically. It suffers further from the effect of a tenor Siegfried cast as a bass Hagen.
GEORGE JEAN NATHAN *NEW YORK JOURNAL-AMERICAN*

THE RETURN OF THE PRODIGAL – 1948

*Walter Hudd as Henry Jackson, David Horne as Samuel Jackson
and John Gielgud as Eustace Jackson in St John Hankin's*
The Return of the Prodigal, *directed by Peter Glenville at the
Globe Theatre.*

There are times when it feels as if *The Return of the Prodigal* has nothing to say which Oscar Wilde did not say far better. However, though St John Hankin was writing in the then fashionable, almost compulsory, epigrammatic manner of his day, he was, in his radical thinking, much nearer to Bernard Shaw and Harley Granville-Barker, whose 1905 Court Theatre season he shared.

The major mistake this revival made was to let Cecil Beaton loose on his favourite period. The play could not be seen for the dressing. The cynicism and disillusionment, which would lead Hankin to take his own life in 1909, was lost in all the theatrical plumage.

Gielgud, as the bone-idle prodigal who threatens to take himself off to the workhouse unless his parvenu family gives him a proper allowance, acted with engaging Saki-esque cheek. The only thing missing from the performance (very much in his best High Comedy manner) was Hankin's bitter denouncement of society, a key speech which had been cut.

Mr Gielgud is prodigal indeed in wasting his substance on a part that calls for little more than slick gaiety and a certain impudent charm.
STEPHEN WILLIAMS *EVENING NEWS*

THE LADY'S NOT FOR BURNING –
1949

Claire Bloom as Alizon Eliot, Nora Nicholson as Margaret Devize, John Gielgud as Thomas Mendip, Pamela Brown as Jennet Jourdemayne, David Evans as Nicholas Devize, Harcourt Williams as Hebble Tyson, Richard Burton as Richard and Richard Leech as Humphrey Devize in Christopher Fry's The Lady's Not for Burning, *directed by John Gielgud and Esmé Percy at the Globe Theatre.*

THE LADY'S NOT FOR BURNING, Christopher Fry's most popular play, belongs to the short-lived renaissance of English verse drama in the immediate post-war years – a renaissance strangled at birth by the arrival of the kitchen-sink drama; though it could easily be argued that Thomas Mendip, and not Jimmy Porter, was the first of all those angry young men who were to rage in the 1950s.

Mendip, a bitter and disenchanted soldier, returning from the wars in Flanders, finds life so grotesque that he confesses to a murder that hasn't been committed and demands to be hanged – until he falls in love with a lady accused of witchcraft.

Gielgud played this romantic, medieval, metaphysical, frolic as if it were a first cousin to an artificial comedy. The verse glimmered and glittered in the second act duet, notable for its lyric beauty and wit.

(overleaf) Pamela Brown as Jennet Jourdemayne and John Gielgud as Thomas Mendip in The Lady's Not for Burning. *(The face in the window is Christopher Fry.)*

1950s

John Gielgud as Jaffeir and Eileen Herlie as Belvidera in Venice Preserv'd 1953.

I feel I have known John all my life: actually I have only known him for something over fifty years. In all that time I have been entirely devoted to him – as I am sure is every actor and actress who has had the joy of working with him.
I have countless reasons for being grateful to John. The first is for his acting – and specifically at the Old Vic in 1930; I saw those performances and they determined me to try and follow in his footsteps. Next I am grateful to him for taking a big risk and throwing himself wholeheartedly into the work at Stratford and playing a major part in some great days there. Most of all, perhaps, I am grateful to him for being such a brave, endlessly amusing, companion, such a warm and generous friend.

ANTHONY QUAYLE

MEASURE FOR MEASURE – 1950

John Gielgud as Angelo and Barbara Jefford as Isabella in Shakespeare's Measure for Measure, *directed by Peter Brook at the Memorial Theatre, Stratford-upon-Avon.*

Peter Brook's brilliant production, which marked Gielgud's debut at Stratford, put this much neglected play back firmly on the theatrical map.

There were those who thought, mistakenly, that Gielgud would have preferred to have played the Duke (a role, incidentally, no actor of the first rank has ever wanted to play) but he had always coveted Angelo, ever since he had seen Charles Laughton play him at the Old Vic in the 1930s. He was, as might be expected, less coarse than Laughton, more aesthetic: a tight-lipped, snow-broth study in sexual repression. His portrait of this proud, aloof man, dress'd in a little brief authority, was painted with icy, cruel intelligence.

Mr Gielgud's Angelo is a very fine performance. Not the least of its virtues is the actor's recognition that Angelo, though dead keen on seducing Isabella, has had very little practice at this sort of thing before – a handicap at which Mr Gielgud percipiently hints in his initial approach to the problem.
PETER FLEMING *SPECTATOR*

JULIUS CAESAR – 1950

John Gielgud as Cassius in Shakespeare's Julius Caesar, *directed by Anthony Quayle and Michael Langham at the Memorial Theatre, Stratford-upon-Avon.*

There has been endless discussion as to whether Brutus or Antony is the hero of the play. At Stratford there never was any doubt. It was Cassius who bestrode the production like a colossus. Gielgud was the driving force, the sheer vigour and vehemence of his passion taking many, including himself, by surprise on the first night.

At the premiere I knew that all was safe with the evening as soon as John Gielgud's Cassius began to urge Brutus to the edge. This scene proved to be one of the noblest feats of declamation in my experience. Though I recognised Gielgud's quality as a Shakespearian, I did not expect this leaping blaze of speech. He has been the principal violin of our stage. Here now, as Cassius, he moves like the Coronation trumpets of the Abbey.
J.C. TREWIN *ILLUSTRATED LONDON NEWS*

MUCH ADO ABOUT NOTHING – 1950

John Gielgud as Benedict and Peggy Ashcroft as Beatrice in Shakespeare's Much Ado About Nothing, *directed by John Gielgud at the Memorial Theatre, Stratford-upon-Avon.*

GIELGUD, perhaps, would not be most people's first choice for Benedict, the professional misogynist, but by concentrating on the witty courtier, rather than the bluff soldier, he made the part peculiarly his own; and such was his personal success, and the success of his production (handsomely designed by Mariano Andreu) that he would continue to fight 'the merry war', off and on, for the next six years, with three different leading ladies.

The raillery had the lightest of touches. Benedict and Beatrice were the most elegant of ballroom dancers, the Fred Astaire and Ginger Rogers of Messina.

KING LEAR – 1950

Maxine Audley as Goneril, John Gielgud as Lear and Gwen Ffrangcon-Davies as Regan in Shakespeare's King Lear, *directed by John Gielgud and Anthony Quayle, with acknowledgements to the late Harley Granville-Barker, at the Memorial Theatre, Stratford-upon-Avon.*

THIS WAS the third of Gielgud's Lears and for many it was the least impressive and most disappointing; though, interestingly, those critics, like Philip Hope-Wallace and T.C. Worsley, who went a second time, were notably more enthusiastic than their colleagues who had attended only the first night.

No one with Gielgud's vocal magnificence could fail to make an effect, but we were hardly shaken as we should have been by the Promethean figure of the storm: indeed we are seldom pierced by Lear's distracted majesty.
IVOR BROWN *OBSERVER*

It is the pathos of a Don Quixote grievously deceived, rather than of a god magnificently overthrown, and in one scene, pictorially, it had a wonderful effect. This is the storm. Amid the thunder and the lightning, Mr Gielgud, against flashing skies, appears tall and gaunt and incredibly elongated, like an El Greco Christ amidst the wreckage of a ruined universe.
HAROLD HOBSON *SUNDAY TIMES*

King Lear is an Ancient Monument; and I am afraid that, in the early stages of the Stratford-upon-Avon revival, that fine actor John Gielgud behaves like a guide who is showing us round.
J.C. TREWIN *JOHN O'LONDON'S WEEKLY*

This is a great Lear.
ALAN DENT *NEWS CHRONICLE*

THE WINTER'S TALE – 1951

Diana Wynyard as Hermione and John Gielgud as Leontes in Shakespeare's The Winter's Tale, *directed by Peter Brook at the Phoenix Theatre.*

T HE WINTER'S TALE is rarely performed; and rarely popular when it is. In the last fifty years, there have been only two successful productions: Peter Brook's in 1951 and Trevor Nunn's in 1969.

Leontes's jealousy is as real and as terrible as Othello's, yet it comes so early on (the play has scarcely begun) as to catch not only Hermione and Polixenes on the hop but the audience as well. Gielgud immediately riveted attention; there was no doubt that he had 'drunk and seen the spider'.

The remorse and reconciliation were beautifully acted. That moment, when Diana Wynyard (the most lovely of statues) stepped down off her pedestal, was truly magical.

Until he played Angelo in Measure for Measure *at Stratford last year, he seemed unable to liberate himself from a certain softness, which derived, I suspect, from a romantic actor's besetting fault of feeling it essential to win the sympathy of an audience. Freed from that restriction, he is now discovering in himself new depths of feeling and ranges of voice, which did not seem to be there before.*
T.C. WORSLEY *NEW STATESMAN AND NATION*

It is a virtuoso performance, theatrically expert in conception and execution and the verse is spoken with subtle lucidity and delicate balance. But this is something more than a technical feat: it has the profundity of common experience, lit by the incandescent fire of maturing genius.
RICHARD FINDLATER *TRIBUNE*

John always went to see new plays and was a great encourager of the young. When I was in an early play of Christopher Fry's he came, and wrote to me – one of his elegant and charming notes. I was very thrilled and touched, and even more so when shortly afterwards he asked me to play Hero in his brilliant production of 'Beatrice and Benedict'. I was very dismal in the part, but what made my evening was watching John from the wings. Not perfectly cast, he played it perfectly. It was so funny. The less he did the better he became – it was a great mystery and total magic.
Years later I watched him rehearse the 'reputation' scene in Othello, the natural lyricism of his style becoming pared down under the naturalistic direction of Zeffirelli. It became more and more simple, and unbearably moving. Peggy Ashcroft and I turned to each other in tears. Privileged we were to see such beauty in acting; but it was made more memorable because the first night was, for various reasons, pretty well a disaster, the natural style of the production clashing with the operatic style of the sets. On the second night there was John, who should have triumphed, not well reviewed – nor any of us – showing a total lack of self-pity. He picked up the play and carried the performance and us along with him, without fuss, but with natural grace and courage. It was an inspiration.
DOROTHY TUTIN

MUCH ADO ABOUT NOTHING – 1952

Penelope Munday as Margaret, John Gielgud as Benedict, Margaret Wolfit as Ursula, Hugh Stewart as Antonio, Dorothy Tutin as Hero, Robert Hardy as Claudio, Diana Wynyard as Beatrice and Lewis Casson as Leonato in Shakespeare's Much Ado About Nothing, *directed by John Gielgud at the Phoenix Theatre.*

MUCH ADO ABOUT NOTHING returned in triumph, its wit unimpaired. Benedict's soliloquy, in which he determines to be *horribly* in love with Beatrice, attempting to justify his turnabout with a remark to the effect that 'When I said I would die a bachelor, I did not think I should live till I were married', was sheer delight from beginning to end.

Mr Gielgud shows once more that it is nonsense to regard him as a tragedian who jokes with difficulty. The truth is that he turns his minor failings as a tragedian, his natural hauteur and air of remoteness, into comic virtues.

THE TIMES

THE WAY OF THE WORLD – 1953

Mairhi Russell as Mincing, Paul Scofield as Witwoud, Pamela Brown as Millamant, John Gielgud as Mirabell and Pauline Jameson as Mrs Fainall in William Congreve's The Way of the World, *directed by John Gielgud at the Lyric Theatre, Hammersmith.*

The Way of the World, sometimes thought to be the wittiest play in the English language (though only when people forget *The Importance of Being Earnest*), has been, ever since its first performance in 1700, a brilliant failure.

Despite its frequent revival, it still comes as a surprise just how small a part Millamant and Mirabell actually do play in this mercenary and sexual cabal. The witty lovers, in effect, share but two scenes. The famous one, in which they lay down their *provisos* for marriage, is the quintessence of Restoration Comedy:

Let us be very strange and well bred. Let us be very strange as if we had been marry'd a great while; and as well bred as if we were not marry'd at all.

The two roles, however, are not, as Beatrice and Benedict are, equally rewarding, and Gielgud, speaking Congreve's polished prose incomparably, found little to do with Mirabell other than be stylish.

The Way of the World is Millamant's play, though in this production she was superseded by the 'superannuated frippery' of Margaret Rutherford's definitive Lady Wishfort, unforgettable in her comedy, pathos and rage.

VENICE PRESERV'D – 1953

John Gielgud as Jaffeir and Eileen Herlie as Belvidera in Thomas Otway's Venice Preserv'd, *directed by Peter Brook at the Lyric Theatre, Hammersmith.*

Venice preserv'd, a once highly popular Restoration Tragedy, acted by Garrick and Mrs Cibber, Kemble and Sarah Siddons, had held the stage for a century and a half, the perfect companion-piece to Lord Byron's *Marino Faliero*.

Peter Brook's production was its first revival in thirty-three years. Gielgud, in his curtain speech, said that he hoped they had turned a museum piece into a collector's item. The play proved an artistic though not a commercial success and would not be seen again for another thirty-three years, not until Peter Gill's Zoffany-heroic production, at the National Theatre, which emphasised the homosexuality of the two conspirators.

Otway based his story on an actual plot to overthrow the Venetian Senate in 1618. Jaffeir, the hero-turned-traitor, a Brutus-like character, in a play which often recalls *Julius Caesar*, is a wavering spirit, a man of many moods and divided loyalties, who finally betrays his friends. The cloak-and-dagger action had an undeniably stagey theatricality and built to an exciting climax in which Jaffeir stabs his best friend Pierre (Paul Scofield) to death to save him from the wrack. Kenneth Tynan thought it would have been wonderful, *pace* the 1935 *Romeo and Juliet*, if Gielgud and Scofield had been able to alternate the two roles.

The high-blown and largely empty rhetoric, which owes more to the French classical tradition than it does to the English theatre, was nobly spoken.

As I write I can hear John's voice ringing down the corridor of the Haymarket calling 'Mac!' He was in his dressing-room, in front of his mirror, impatiently putting on his make-up and I was a student from Oxford, who had managed to slip past the stage door man to make a request to the great man. 'We're making an undergraduate film and were wondering if you could let us film a scene in the set of Love for Love. You see, we need —' But I did not need to finish the sentence. John had already called out 'Mac!', and as his devoted dresser arrived he was already giving instructions for us to be given everything we needed. This was a start of a lifelong friendship and my first experience of those lighting impulses, those generous flashes, that so define John the artist and John the man.

PETER BROOK

JULIUS CAESAR – 1953

John Gielgud as Cassius and James Mason as Brutus in the film version of Shakespeare's Julius Caesar, *directed by Joseph L. Mankiewicz.*

Though John Houseman, the producer, described *Julius Caesar* as 'a political thriller', there were, with the exception of the actual murder, very few thrills, and despite some impressive acting – James Mason's noble Brutus, in particular, (a much underrated performance) – the film remained curiously lifeless. It was as if an audience had been invited to watch some well-rehearsed scenes from a stage production. The crowd scenes in the Roman Forum and the Battle of Philippi were shamefully ineffectual.

Gielgud arrived in Hollywood with the tremendous advantage of knowing his part, having just acted the play at Stratford-upon-Avon. His Cassius – astute, dangerous, neurotic and petty – won him the Best British Actor of the Year Award from the British Film Academy.

For those cinemagoers who wondered why Marlon Brando's magnetic Antony was so much more confident with the speech over Caesar's dead body than he was with the more famous one in the Forum (where Shakespeare's syntax gave him considerable trouble) the answer might well have been that he was coached by Gielgud in the first, but not the second.

A DAY BY THE SEA – 1953

*Irene Worth as Frances Farrar, Peter Murphy as Toby Eddison,
Ralph Richardson as Doctor Farley, Sybil Thorndike as Laura
Anson, Frederick Piper as William Gregson, Patricia Laurence as
Elinor Eddison, Megs Jenkins as Miss Mathieson, John Gielgud
as Julian Anson, Lockwood West as Humphrey Caldwell and
Lewis Casson as David Anson in N.C. Hunter's* A Day by the Sea,
directed by John Gielgud at the Theatre Royal, Haymarket.

N C. HUNTER's melancholy mood-piece – wistful,
gentle, bitter studies in loneliness, frustration, lost
opportunities and unfulfilled ambitions – was very much
in the Chekhov idiom and offered a distinguished cast
excellent possibilities for some fine ensemble playing.

Gielgud, taut and restless, was cast as the dreary son
of the house, a failed diplomat, who proposes twenty
years too late to a woman who already has had two
disastrous marriages and is not keen to have a third.

A Day by the Sea was one of Gielgud's finest
productions.

STARS AT MIDNIGHT – 1953

Laurence Olivier, John Mills and John Gielgud in Stars at
Midnight, *a midnight charity show at the Palladium Theatre.
The actors are seen here singing Noel Coward's lyric*
Three Not-so-Juvenile Delinquents.

KING LEAR – 1955

*Claire Bloom as Cordelia and John Gielgud as Lear in
Shakespeare's* King Lear, *directed by George Devine, for the
Shakespeare Memorial Theatre Company, at the Palace Theatre.*

SHAKESPEARE and the actors fought a losing battle
with Isamu Noguchi's designs for the audience's
attention. The designs would have been more appropriate for a Martha Graham ballet. There were Martian
soldiers, Japanese swords, triangular shapes (some of
them apt to get up and move about the stage), suspended
bits of abstract scenery, an artist's giant palate for Kent's
stocks, and what looked like a lavatory seat, though, as it
was not used, it may not have been. As for Lear, he was
so fantastically dressed, the holes in his garments getting
larger and larger, that when the moment came that he
should enter dressed fantastically, the designer had to
put him into something really quite respectable having by
then torn his garments to shreds. Gielgud played Lear as
if he were playing Gloucester.

Lear looks like a Gruyère cheese.
HAROLD CONWAY *DAILY SKETCH HEADLINE*

*This is not his part at all. He lacks the sheer dynamic
necessary to carry it off. Lear is a Titan or nothing.
Anything that falls short of that is worse than useless, and
Sir John is not Titanic. His rage in the storm, in spite of his
voice and his mastery of Shakespearian verse rhythms, fell
far short of a man identifying himself with the elements
and celebrating the feast of nature's unrule. We were not
transported by this frenzy.*
ANTHONY HARTLEY *SPECTATOR*

RICHARD III – 1955

John Gielgud as Clarence, Mary Kerridge as Queen Elizabeth, Cedric Hardwicke as Edward IV, Paul Huson as Prince Edward and Laurence Olivier as Gloucester in the film version of Shakespeare's Richard III, *directed by Laurence Olivier.*

GIELGUD, as false, fleeting, perjur'd Clarence, was no 'quicksand of deceit' but unexpectedly sensitive and gentle, his eyes filling with tears at the coronation ceremony.

His memorable, quite unforgettable phrasing of the famous lines, in which he so vividly recounts his terrible dream of death by drowning, was universally praised, and would later become one of the highlights of his Shakespearian recital, *Ages of Man*.

AROUND THE WORLD IN 80 DAYS – 1956

Noel Coward as Roland Hesketh-Baggott, John Gielgud as Foster and Cantinflas as Passepartout in Jules Verne's Around the World in 80 Days, *a film directed by Michael Anderson.*

GIELGUD and Coward were just two in an army of famous actors who were enlisted to play bit parts in Mike Todd's 4,000,000 dollar spectacular.

Audiences did not come to see if Phileas Fogg (played by David Niven) would win his bet. They came to spot the stars. Blink and they might miss six. There was so little urgency about the film that it would have served Fogg right if he had lost his bet.

Gielgud played a disgruntled, out-of-work gentleman's gentleman, the first of his many screen valets.

NUDE WITH VIOLIN – 1956

Patience Collier as Anya Pavlikov, David Horne as Jacob Friedland and John Gielgud as Sebastien in Noel Coward's Nude with Violin, *directed by John Gielgud and Noel Coward at the Globe Theatre.*

NUDE WITH VIOLIN, a feeble joke at the expense of the art world, was about a famous painter who, on the day of his funeral, is found to have been a complete fraud. He had never painted anything in his life, his masterpieces having been painted for him by a Russian princess, a cockney chorus girl, a Jamaican Seventh Day Adventist and a schoolboy.

Gielgud played the dead man's resourceful valet, a suave blackmailer, a latter-day Mosca, bringing multilingual polish to an underwritten part, originally intended for Rex Harrison and very nearly played by Yvonne Arnaud.

Coward got a terrible press, which didn't make a scrap of difference to the box office receipts, and when Gielgud left the cast his role was taken first by Michael Wilding and then by Robert Helpmann.

Sir John never acts seriously in modern dress; it is the lounging attire in which he relaxes between classical bookings; and his present performance as a simpering valet is an act of boyish mischief, carried out with extreme elegance and the general aspect of a tight, smart, walking umbrella.

KENNETH TYNAN *OBSERVER*

THE TEMPEST – 1957

Richard Johnson as Ferdinand, John Gielgud as Prospero and Doreen Aris as Miranda in Shakespeare's The Tempest, *directed by Peter Brook at the Shakespeare Memorial Theatre, Stratford-upon-Avon. The production transferred to the Theatre Royal, Drury Lane.*

Sir John Gielgud, of course, has all the qualities for Prospero. He is, above all, the speaking poet of our theatre and here, appearing in the handsome stamp of an Old Testament prophet in the wilderness, he speaks the poetry with an enthralling appreciation for its sense and music.
DEREK GRANGER *FINANCIAL TIMES*

Bodily inexpressive and manually gauche, he is perhaps the finest actor, from the neck up, in the world today. His face is all rigour and pain; his voice all 'cello and woodwind; the rest of him is totem-pole. But he speaks the great passages perfectly, and always looks full of thinking. The part demands no more.
KENNETH TYNAN *OBSERVER*

THE BARRETTS OF WIMPOLE STREET – 1957

Virginia McKenna as Henrietta, Jennifer Jones as Elizabeth Barrett and John Gielgud as Edward Moulton Barrett in The Barretts of Wimpole Street, *a film directed by Sidney Franklin.*

THE CARELESS rapture of Elizabeth and Robert Browning, the petty tyrannies of the father, and the sickly sentimentality of the scenes round the day-bed, all had a deadening, badly acted 1930s theatricality.

Barrett's incestuous feelings for his daughter were so tactfully expressed that the censor missed them completely and awarded the film a 'U' certificate. Far more shocking was the admission that only the first of his seven children had been conceived in love and that the other six had all been conceived in fear.

Gielgud, in an overwritten part, was constantly hav-ing to make melodramatic entrances. His most memor-able line – certainly his biggest laugh – was when he caught Henrietta with her uniformed beau. 'Since when has it been your custom to button on his accoutrements?' he asked.

SAINT JOAN – 1957

Harry Andrews as de Stogumber and John Gielgud as the Earl of Warwick in the film version of Bernard Shaw's Saint Joan, *directed by Otto Preminger.*

OTTO PREMINGER'S mistake was to cast an inexperi-enced eighteen-year-old to play Joan. Poor Jean Seberg, having nearly been burnt at the stake during the shooting, got a further roasting from the critics on the film's release. The role of Warwick was much truncated.

THE POTTING SHED – 1958

Irene Worth as Sara Callifer, Lockwood West as John Callifer, Walter Hudd as Dr Frederick Baston, Sarah Long as Anne Callifer, Gwen Ffrangcon-Davies as Mrs Callifer and John Gielgud as James Callifer in Graham Greene's The Potting Shed, *directed by Michael MacOwan at the Globe Theatre.*

GRAHAM GREENE's play is a spiritual detective story in which a Nottingham journalist, searching for the cause of his deep-seated misery, discovers that when he was fourteen-years-old he hanged himself, in the potting shed, and was given up for dead. His uncle, a Roman Catholic priest, prayed to God, and much to the consternation of his family, all good atheists, the boy was raised from the dead.

By far the best scene, certainly the most controversial, was the one in which the journalist visits his uncle, now a broken old man, who remembers the day the boy died and the pact he made with God: 'Let him live . . . I will give you anything . . . take away what I love most . . . take away my faith.'

Gielgud expertly conveyed the anguish and anxiety of a modern-day Lazarus, while Redmond Phillips, as the priest, walked off with the play.

The play is certainly not Catholic propaganda, as so many critics think.
                                        CATHOLIC HERALD

Having known J.G. and worked with him over so many years there is much one would like to say – suffice it to say he has always been such an example and inspiration to other actors of my generation as well as a very dear friend to me. I owe much to him in my career and it has always been a delight to work with him either as actor or director.

There are many anecdotes, of course, that one could remember. One that is typical of him and his relationship with me was when he was directing his first production of his famous Much Ado About Nothing at Stratford in 1949. He was busy playing in something on tour and had only limited time to direct us. A few days before dress rehearsals, he decided to alter completely an important scene in which I, as Don Pedro, was very much involved. This is something anyone who has been directed by John is liable to dread, particularly me! In front of the company I stamped my foot and said: 'John, surely you know me well enough to know that I can't cope with this sort of thing at this stage of the production.' His immediate response was to say: 'Oh yes, of course, Harry, you are rather slow, aren't you? All right then, just do it your way.' And that was that.

I treasure so many happy memories of him, the greatest poetic actor and man of the theatre of our age – bless him.

HARRY ANDREWS

HENRY VIII – 1958

Harry Andrews as Henry and John Gielgud as Cardinal Wolsey in Shakespeare's Henry VIII, *directed by Michael Benthall at the Old Vic Theatre.*

Henry VIII is immensely boring Tudor propaganda and should, perhaps, be restricted to royal occasions. The only successful revival in recent times has been Tyrone Guthrie's production, also for the Old Vic Company, in Coronation Year 1953, when a loyal public was able to punctuate Archbishop Cranmer's patriotic speech to a new Elizabethan Age with patriotic applause.

Gielgud's Wolsey, neither vulgar nor fat (even with padding) was no 'butcher's cur' but rather a 'high-nosed ascetic', most at ease in the long farewell to his greatness, a famous set-piece in which Shakespeare attempts to raise the Cardinal to tragic heights without any preparation.

THE BROWNING VERSION – 1959

Margaret Leighton as Millie Crocker-Harris and John Gielgud as Andrew Crocker-Harris in Terence Rattigan's The Browning Version, *directed by John Frankenheimer for CBS.*

GIELGUD scored a major triumph, in his American television debut, as the failed public schoolmaster, the Himmler of the Lower Fifth – a role, Rattigan had specially written for him, and which he, to Rattigan's mortification, turned down when the play was first produced in the West End.

The scene, when the pupil Taplow gives him a gift of Browning's version of Aeschylus' *Agamemnon*, was particularly moving.

A DAY BY THE SEA – 1959

John Gielgud as Julian Anson and Roger Livesey as Doctor Farley in N.C. Hunter's A Day by the Sea, *directed by Lionel Harris for BBC Television.*

GIELGUD decided, that for his English TV debut, he would prefer to be seen in a modern part and doing one that he knew well and had lived with for a long time in a successful West End run.

A Day by the Sea did not translate well to the small screen and most people were disappointed that he had not chosen something meatier than pastiche Chekhov.

AGES OF MAN – 1959

John Gielgud in his one-man show, Shakespeare's Ages of Man, based on George Rylands's Shakespeare Anthology, at the Queen's Theatre.

John Gielgud offers us climaxes without preparation, an impossible task which he accomplished triumphantly. Contravening the sound assumption that you cannot get to the top of a mountain without climbing first, Sir John throughout the evening appears on one summit of Shakespeare's verse after another, without ever descending to the intervening valleys.
HAROLD HOBSON *SUNDAY TIMES*

What is so admirable about Sir John is that he places his gifts – of voice, intelligence, of understanding, of sympathy – completely at the service of the work he is interpreting.
T.C. WORSLEY *FINANCIAL TIMES*

Here is a testament to the power and beauty of the word in an age when scenery so often dominates the productions of Shakespeare.
RICHARD FINDLATER *SUNDAY DISPATCH*

Those who have not seen Sir John in Shakespeare should run to hear how great words can ring out, for I do not know who after him is to carry on the tradition.
RONALD MAVOR *SCOTSMAN*

I find King Lear in a bow-tie distracting.
MILTON SHULMAN *EVENING STANDARD*

1960s

John Gielgud as Joseph Surface in The School for Scandal *1962.*

THE LAST JOKE – 1960

Robert Fleming as Hugo Vavanti, Ralph Richardson as Edward Portal, John Gielgud as Prince Ferdinand Cavanati, Robin Hawdon as Robin, Ernest Thesiger as Baron Santa Clara and Anna Massey as Rose in Enid Bagnold's The Last Joke, *directed by Glen Byam Shaw at the Phoenix Theatre.*

Tʜᴇ Lᴀsᴛ Jᴏᴋᴇ, based on incidents in Enid Bagnold's early life, should have been played as a period piece. The play, which arrived in London, after much tinkering with the text, acted like an early Anouilh, but was fatally uncertain whether it was a *pièce rose* or a *pièce noir*. The production pleased nobody, the author least of all.

Gielgud was cast as a Romanian aristocrat who threatens to commit suicide. It was difficult to care whether he did or not. Enid Bagnold had wanted him to play the millionaire, the role Richardson played.

OTHELLO – 1961

John Gielgud as Othello in Shakespeare's Othello, *directed by Franco Zeffirelli at the Royal Shakespeare Theatre, Stratford-upon-Avon.*

Tʜᴇ Iᴛᴀʟɪᴀɴ ᴅɪʀᴇᴄᴛᴏʀ, Franco Zeffirelli, had scored a big success with *Romeo and Juliet* at the Old Vic, with John Stride and Judi Dench as the star-cross'd lovers. It had been one of the most important and innovative Shakespearian productions since the war; so his failure with *Othello* was felt all the more keenly.

Gielgud could never have been a natural for the Moor, being neither believable as a great soldier, nor as a great lover. The production had a disastrous first night. The backstage staff had enormous difficulty moving the monumental scenery. There were endless pauses between scenes, pillars wobbled, beards came off, lines were forgot and Iago told the world that Cassio was dead (much to the surprise of Cassio who was in the wings, waiting to come on). When Othello came to the line *Chaos is come again*, he was merely voicing what everybody else had been thinking all evening.

Gielgud himself is quite simply over-parted. In his hands Othello dwindles into a coffee-stained Leontes; instead of a wounded bull, dangerous despite its injuries, we have a heraldic eagle with its wings harmlessly clipped.
KENNETH TYNAN *OBSERVER*

Far from suggesting that he could eat Desdemona raw for breakfast, he makes one feel he would really like her served on a tray in the library.
PENELOPE GILLIATT *QUEEN*

Gielgud, trying to rise above the admonishment with dignity, was very funny.

There was also that perfect Chekhovian moment when Gaev returns from the auction, the orchard having been sold, weeping profusely while carrying some absurdly dainty parcels of bons-bons; he managed to be both tragic and farcical at the same time.

THE CHERRY ORCHARD – 1961

Dorothy Tutin as Varya, John Gielgud as Gaev and Judi Dench as Anya in Anton Chekhov's The Cherry Orchard, *directed by Michel Saint-Denis for the Royal Shakespeare Company at the Aldwych Theatre.*

MICHEL SAINT-DENIS's somewhat broad production was compared unfavourably with the one the Moscow Arts Theatre had brought to London in 1958. The teamwork of the Russians, the naturalism of their acting, the lighting (especially the dawn in the first act) and the political force of Trofimov, a perpetual student who really did believe in the future – all these things had deeply impressed the theatrical profession.

Gaev is one of Chekhov's most endearing characters: a dear, kind, silly, boring old man who talks all the time, even to the bookcase. His scenes with Firs were delightful. 'What am I going to do with you, eh?' asks the old retainer, adopting a tone more appropriate when dealing with a little boy rather than a grown man.

THE CHERRY ORCHARD – 1962

Peggy Ashcroft as Mme Ranevsky and John Gielgud as Gaev in Anton Chekhov's The Cherry Orchard, *directed by Michel Saint-Denis for the Royal Shakespeare Company, presented by BBC Television.*

THE SCHOOL FOR SCANDAL –
1962

John Gielgud as Joseph Surface, Ralph Richardson as Sir Peter Teazle and Geraldine McEwan as Lady Teazle in Richard Brinsley Sheridan's The School for Scandal, *directed by John Gielgud at the Theatre Royal, Haymarket. The production transferred to the Majestic Theatre, New York.*

GIELGUD returned to one of his most celebrated roles, after a twenty-five-year interval, when his production was recast for its North American tour.

Sir John has a natural instinctive feeling for the kind of civilised sharpness which lies not so much in the wit as in the shape of Sheridan's lines. While others make one conscious of the lack of substance, Sir John makes every sentence seem to carry twice its weight by phrasing it so perfectly. It is the very model of how this language should be spoken.
T.C. WORSLEY *FINANCIAL TIMES*

By slightly raising a corner of his mouth, and distending the left nostril, he can express a cargo of contempt better than some actors can in fifty lines.
NORMAN NADEL *NEW YORK WORLD-TELEGRAM*

THE IDES OF MARCH – 1963

John Gielgud as Julius Caesar and John Stride as Valerius Catullus in Jerome Kilty's The Ides of March, *based on the novel by Thornton Wilder, directed by John Gielgud and Jerome Kilty at the Theatre Royal, Haymarket.*

JEROME KILTY had had considerable success in adapting the letters of Bernard Shaw and Mrs Patrick Campbell for the stage in *Dear Liar*; but his attempt to turn Thornton Wilder's imagined correspondence between Caesar, Cleopatra, Cuttulus, Clodia and Brutus into a play failed completely.

The production was mounted in a mixture of modern and Roman dress. Gielgud, wearing a laurel leaf, and a toga over his lounge suit, was seen dipping into a *Penguin* to read a description of his own death by Suetonius.

Here is an SOS. Will Sir John Gielgud, now believed to be wasting his great talent at the Haymarket, please return at once to the theatre of Shakespeare, where his admirers are dangerously restive.

GERALD BARRY *PUNCH*

TINY ALICE – 1964

Irene Worth as Miss Alice and John Gielgud as Julian in Edward Albee's Tiny Alice, *directed by Alan Schneider at the Billy Rose Theatre, New York.*

TINY ALICE, a mixture of religious and sexual ecstasy, was a metaphysical and conventional mystery, which three of New York's leading critics admitted they did not understand and could not describe. They were not the only ones to be baffled and exasperated.

Julian was a lay-brother, who had lost his faith and now worked as secretary for a cardinal. Alice was the richest woman in the world and she was willing to pay good money for a good lay.

I was unhappy in it. I never understood what Albee was saying in the third act. I don't think any of us did . . . He never would discuss the play with me and I never could find any indication of what he wanted.

JOHN GIELGUD

If your lucky star leads you to Venice when John is there and the city is empty of tourists, he will take you on a tour at night to show you the buildings and vistas and outdoor sculpture he loves best. He has a profound love of architecture and a piercing eye. This taste also pervades his personal life so that the houses he lives in have great warmth and allure about them. His present garden in the country is large, simple, classically drawn, surrounded by smaller, charming gardens, created by the superb Martin Hensler. On autumn days John is to be found making a huge bonfire. He has surrendered to the country.

He practises and performs his roles by the rules of classical discipline and these have made him the romantic actor of such unique spirit. He is universally loved now as a modern actor as well but he never oversteps the line which intrudes.

When we were on tour in a recital of Shakespeare I once said to him: 'When you speak that sonnet you make it so accessible. How do you do it?' John said: 'I just follow the beat. It's obscure but the rhythm makes it clear.'

He follows the beat, he is clear. His mind works at lightning speed, his energy is positive, he relies on his strength. He is never idle, he is never ill. He is prompt. He replies to all letters, he has time for everything, he learns his roles by writing them out in his fine, nearly illegible longhand.

John has an undiminished curiosity and interest in the theatre, in new actors, writers, directors; he searches them out like truffles. He remembers the names of all his colleagues from time immemorial. 'That's so and so, he was with me in –' then follows play, date and theatre. Historians will find it hard to convey his grace as a host, that particular atmosphere of excitement, contentment, refined good living, fantastic talk and enjoyment all presided over by the descant of John's youth, jokes, eagerness and puns. The conversations have acquired epic reputations. Less obvious are his qualities of character which have given him such stature. He has reserves of commitment and fairness, patience and equilibrium and endurance.

His agreeable nature and his humility give him resilience. He is a radiant man and a rare friend.

IRENE WORTH

BECKET – 1964

Richard Burton as Becket and John Gielgud as Louis VII in the film version of Jean Anouilh's Becket, *directed by Peter Glenville.*

GIELGUD played the wily King of France with great charm, elegance and wit. He was nominated for an 'Oscar'.

THE LOVED ONE – 1965

John Gielgud as Sir Francis Hinsley and Robert Morse as Dennis Barlow in the film version of Evelyn Waugh's The Loved One, *directed by Tony Richardson.*

THE LOVED ONE was billed as 'the motion picture with something to offend everybody'. The people most likely to have been offended were those who had come to see Evelyn Waugh. The gross vulgarity (especially those scenes with Jobjoy's mother, played by Ayllene Gibbons with sickening gluttony) had nothing to do with the bad taste of the original. Even more unforgivable was the attempt to improve on the novel's climax.

Sir Francis Hinsley, the old has-been, once the doyen of the British colony in Hollywood, who hangs himself when he is given the push by the studio bosses, could have been a good part, but cut to a cameo and all opportunities for pathos carefully avoided, there wasn't much Gielgud could do with it. He was at his funniest as a corpse, on a mortician's slab, pulling beatific faces at the touch of the embalmer's fingers.

IVANOV – 1965

John Gielgud as Ivanov and Claire Bloom as Sasha in Anton Chekhov's Ivanov, *directed by John Gielgud at the Phoenix Theatre.*

I haven't the heart to believe in anything. I hope for nothing, care for no one. I only dread the thought of waking up each morning.

IVANOV

Ivanov, the impoverished landowner, unable to solve either his financial or his emotional problems, is a weak, indolent, neurotic, middle-aged Hamlet, who prefers to shoot himself rather than go through with a second marriage.

Gielgud caught perfectly the emptiness which is at the very heart of this self-centred, self-pitying and self-despising man, turning the Act III prose soliloquy into poetry, and making much of the scene when Ivanov, brutally and senselessly, tells his ailing Jewish wife that she is dying.

CAMPANADAS A MEDIANOCHE – 1966

John Gielgud as Henry IV in the film version of Shakespeare's Campanadas a Medianoche, *being directed by Orson Welles who also played Falstaff.*
English title: Chimes at Midnight.

CHIMES AT MIDNIGHT – described by Welles as 'a lament for the death of Merrie England' – was based on passages from *Richard II*, *Henry IV Parts I and II*, *Henry V* and *The Merry Wives of Windsor*.

The film, an essay on the relationship between Falstaff and the future King of England, was best appreciated by those who knew their Shakespeare well. The chopping, changing, transposing of whole scenes from their context, and the dubbing, did not always make for true clarity; though as an exercise in how to do things when you have no money, the film was an object lesson in economy. Welles relied almost entirely on close-up, even in the Battle of Shrewsbury, superbly edited.

Gielgud had wanted to do the *play* with Ralph Richardson, but Richardson, understandably, had not been willing to run the risk of repeating Falstaff, his great success in the legendary 1944/45 Old Vic season with Laurence Olivier.

Keith Baxter, playing Hal, seized the opportunity (in his 'mock-interview' with Falstaff when the lines called for him to imitate the king's voice) to caricature *Gielgud's* own familiar vocal mannerisms; it gave an already funny scene an additional in-joke for the profession.

ALICE IN WONDERLAND – 1966

Malcolm Muggeridge as the Gryphon, Anne-Marie Mallik as Alice and John Gielgud as the Mock Turtle in Lewis Carroll's Alice in Wonderland, *directed by Jonathan Miller for BBC Television.*

WHEN Huw Weldon, controller of BBC TV, saw what Jonathan Miller had done with *Alice in Wonderland*, he judged it unsuitable for children and dropped the production from the Christmas schedule.

Miller's interpretation was for an adult audience who knew the original text pretty well. He replaced all the animals with humans. The Gryphon and the Mock Turtle were played as a couple of lackadaisical Victorian uncles. The Tenniel drawings were sorely missed.

TARTUFFE – 1967

John Gielgud as Orgon and Robert Stephens as Tartuffe in Molière's Tartuffe, *directed by Tyrone Guthrie for the National Theatre at the Old Vic Theatre.*

THE MAJOR PROBLEM for any actor playing Orgon (it had been presumed Gielgud would play Tartuffe) is to make Orgon's gullability and infatuation believable; if the religious imposter is acted for outright farce, the task is impossible. Nobody could ever have been taken in by Robert Stephens's crude country yokel. Gielgud wouldn't even have let him into the house.

Nine years later National Theatre audiences were able to see France's Théâtre National Populaire's liberating production, directed by Roger Planchon, which took the play quite seriously and the scene in which Orgon hands over all his wealth to Tartuffe was acted like a scene out of *Othello*. Planchon had been the director Gielgud had wanted to direct him.

SAINT JOAN – 1968

Maurice Denham as Cauchon and John Gielgud as the Inquisitor in Bernard Shaw's Saint Joan, *directed by Waris Hussein for BBC Television. Janet Suzman played Joan.*

IT IS A somewhat pointless exercise to cast Gielgud as the Inquisitor – presumably so that full justice can be done to a long and difficult speech – if three quarters of it is then cut.

Despite the clumsy truncation of his argument, his incredible authority as an actor made everyone else seem paper-thin. It's not that he upstages. He just has to sit there.
GEORGE MELLY *OBSERVER*

THE CHARGE OF THE LIGHT BRIGADE – 1968

John Gielgud as Lord Raglan in The Charge of the Light Brigade, *a film directed by Tony Richardson.*

It will be a sad day when armies are officered by men who know what they are doing.
LORD RAGLAN

THE CHARGE OF THE LIGHT BRIGADE, to which the London critics were not invited, resulting in an enormous amount of much needed free publicity, was a biting satire on the most famous of all British military blunders. The best things about the film were the credit titles and animation sequences by Richard Williams, based on contemporary *Punch* cartoons and *Illustrated London News* engravings.

Lord Raglan, who thought he was still fighting the French, spent much of his time worrying about a huge statue of Wellington which blocked the view from his War Office window. Gielgud's gentle caricature of bumbling ineptitude was as endearing as it was amusing.

The film was a major turning-point in his career in the cinema, leading to an unending supply of scene-stealing cameo roles in a whole series of good, bad and quite appalling films.

OEDIPUS – 1968

*Irene Worth as Jocasta and John Gielgud as Oedipus in Seneca's
Oedipus, directed by Peter Brook, for the National Theatre, at the
Old Vic Theatre.*

There never were any Gods. There is only death.

WHEN the audience entered the theatre, the actors,
in brown sweaters and slacks, were already there,
either on-stage or in the auditorium, tied to the pillars
like prisoners to the mast. (Latecomers used to ask them
for programmes.) The actors on-stage sat on small cubes
while an enormous God-like cube revolved hypnotically.
The audience, if not exactly silenced, was certainly
hushed in expectation of the Holy Ritual to come.

Seneca's version of a familiar story is far more brutal
and far more horrifying than Sophocles', the brutality
and horror underlined in the translation and in Peter
Brook's production, very much a companion piece to his
King Lear, Marat/Sade and *US.*

Gielgud, as Oedipus, built steadily to a climax,
which left him, hands pinioned, body twisted and mouth
gaping wide, in a silent agonised scream, worthy of
Francis Bacon. There was too that magnificent moment
when he realised that it was *he* who had brought destruc-
tion on Thebes and he called on all the diseases and
terrors of mankind to join him in exile.

The verbal and physical agony over, a giant golden
phallus (owner unidentified) was brought on, to the
admiration and applause of the spectators, while the cast
jived away on-stage and in the aisles.

*He wouldn't let me be emotional. He made me stylised and
he wouldn't allow me to let go. I'd been hoping I'd have a
chance to rival Larry's Oedipus with all that screaming
and howling. But Brook's Oedipus was so different, so
staid, so stylised, so static.*
JOHN GIELGUD QUOTED BY NICHOLAS DE JONGH *GUARDIAN*

FROM CHEKHOV WITH LOVE – 1968

Peggy Ashcroft as Olga Knipper, Maurice Denham as Alexander Chekhov, John Gielgud as Anton Chekhov, Dorothy Tutin as Maria, Nigel Davenport as Maxim Gorky and Wendy Hiller as Mme Avilova in From Chekhov With Love, *staged by Jonathan Miller and directed by Bill Turner for Rediffusion Television.*

FROM CHEKHOV WITH LOVE was a portrait of the Russian playwright's life built up through letters from and to him. The production was a series of stylised tableaux.

SEBASTIAN – 1968

John Gielgud as Head of Intelligence and Dirk Bogarde as Sebastian in Sebastian, *a film directed by David Greene.*

SEBASTIAN was a swinging sixties comedy-thriller. The Head of Intelligence was such an unpleasant character that it was a major surprise to find he was not (as is the usual practice in spy films and real life) the villain of the piece, working for the other side.

40 YEARS ON – 1968

John Gielgud as the Headmaster and Alan Bennett as Tempest, a junior master, in Alan Bennett's 40 Years On, directed by Patrick Garland at the Apollo Theatre.

40 YEARS ON, which traced the decline of England from the turn of the century to the Second World War, was acted out within the framework of an end-of-term revue at a very minor public school.

Alan Bennett's affectionate satire was a verbally dextrous mixture of esoteric jokes, blasphemy, misquotation, rugby songs, literary pastiche and schoolboy smut. ('When society has to resort to the lavatory for its humour, the writing's on the wall.')

Gielgud played the retiring headmaster, a pillar to conservatism, in a way which was both comic and touching. The opening rambling address (which combined rhetoric, mumbo-jumbo cliché, admonishment and prayer) was very funny, just as the final lament for an old order – and Edwardian past irrevocably lost – was deeply moving.

He also had two cameo roles: the aged butler to a Wildean dowager and a judge, sitting in a court of history, sentencing Neville Chamberlain to 'perpetual ignominy'.

John Gielgud plays Albion's headmaster, a fastidious, maudlin old spinster, and is at his most elegant, attenuated and mellow, like a Stradivarius playing Mozart.
BENEDICT NIGHTINGALE *NEW STATESMAN*

In his best stage part for years Gielgud shows us what we have been allowed to forget – how splendid a comic actor he is. He speaks absurdities, he makes a dignified ass of himself; and he gives the impression of enjoying himself enormously.
JEREMY KINGSTON *PUNCH*

Gielgud dominates all with an unexpected caricature of a mincing pedant, his noble features blurred so as to mimic a fussed and fatuous egghead. From the great mandarin of the theatre, a delicious comic creation.
JOHN BARBER *DAILY TELEGRAPH*

OH! WHAT A LOVELY WAR – 1969

John Gielgud as Count Leopold von Berchtold in the film version of Joan Littlewood and Charles Hilton's Oh! What A Lovely War, *directed by Richard Attenborough.*

Gielgud was one of many stars who accepted cameo roles so that Richard Attenborough could raise the necessary two-and-a-half million dollars to make *Oh! What A Lovely War.* The film had nothing like the emotional impact of the original stage version; the theatrical conceit, of acting out the satire on the officer class and the terrible carnage of the Great War on the Brighton Pier, just did not work in the cinema.

Count Leopold von Berchtold was the inept Austrian Foreign Minister, a liar, double-dealer, fool, dilettante, who had long been recognised by his countrymen as being 'outstanding for the vacuity of his mind and the snobbishness of his character'.

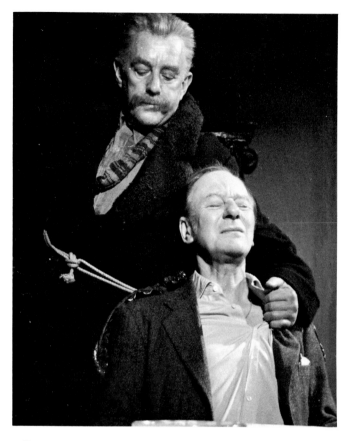

CONVERSATION AT NIGHT – 1969

Alec Guinness as The Executioner and John Gielgud as The Writer in Friedrich Durrenmatt's Conversation at Night, *directed by Rudolph Cartier for BBC Television.*

The conversation, which took place in a totalitarian state, was between an intellectual writer and a philosophical public hangman. The writer had to learn to accept death without rebellion, bitterness or tears.

1970s

John Gielgud as Sir Geoffrey Kendle in Veterans 1972.

THE BATTLE OF SHRIVINGS – 1970

Patrick Magee as Mark and John Gielgud as Gideon in Peter Shaffer's The Battle of Shrivings, *directed by Peter Hall at the Lyric Theatre.*

Gideon is a philosopher-saint, aesthete-vegetarian and President of the World League of Peace. He is challenged to a symbolic duel by an old friend, an ex-pupil, a famous poet. The poet says he will make Gideon hate him so much that he will order him out of the house. The outcome of this intellectual and highly artificial debate is never in any doubt; nevertheless when the world-famous humanist finds he is just as lacking in humanity as everybody else he lets out a howl of despair,

such as could only be heard in a theatre.

The Battle of Shrivings was very wordy, far too long and not nearly dramatic enough. The third act, in particular, was very heavy-going, a real penance for audience and actors alike.

EAGLE IN A CAGE – 1970

John Gielgud as Lord Sissal and Ralph Richardson as Sir Hudson Lowe in Eagle in a Cage, *a film directed by Fielder Cook.*

If I were a woman, I'd be a whore. But since I'm a man, I'm a politician. The Empire is the only mistress I can satisfy now.

LORD SISSAL

Lord Sissal, an emissary from London, arrives in St Helena to offer Napoleon his freedom if he will return to France and head a puppet government.

The cynical, devious Sissal, a rude old Regency rake (a totally fictional character) gave Gielgud plenty of opportunity to turn a cameo role into a star part.

JULIUS CAESAR – 1970

Richard Johnson as Cassius and John Gielgud as Caesar in the film version of Shakespeare's Julius Caesar, *directed by Stuart Burge*

Nobody emerged with any credit from this old-fashioned, unexciting production, mounted on the cheap, with tatty sets and costumes. The film had obviously been directed by somebody who did not know the first thing about cinema; it was so badly shot as to be continually distracting.

He gives a more sensitive rendering than is usually seen – so sensitive that it almost seems as if he rather than Brutus was the noblest Roman of them all.

ALEXANDER WALKER *EVENING STANDARD*

Nothing in John Gielgud's wonderful career is more wonderful, it seems to me, or more exemplary, than his sanguine acceptance of the passing of time and his coming to friendly terms with whole new generations of writers, directors and fellow-artists. Once I (strange to think) represented a young and impatiently critical new generation in the theatre. I had met John several times socially — and had always, I imagined, behaved with a modest discretion, calculated to show the great respect I felt for him. I had failed to understand that every actor, no matter how eminent, needs the reassurance of expressed approval: John, who has pride but no arrogance, was no exception. So I was astonished to be told by Gregori Kozintsev, the Russian director of Hamlet and Lear on film, of John's reaction on being shown the record of Ages of Man, which I had given Kozintsev on a visit to Moscow. 'How extraordinary,' had been John's comment. 'He hates me.'

Of course, I never hated John. I thought of him as a remote, distinguished planet, circling with a certain hauteur, above the contemporary struggle. At that time, I think it's fair to say, he regarded our Royal Court activities with suspicion. None the less, I asked him to play Caesar at the Court, and I distinctly remember walking down Cowley Street on a dark evening and putting my carefully phrased invitation through his letter-box. I never received an answer. At the time I put this down to his reciprocal dislike of me, though John has since denied that he ever received my letter. On reflection, I have to believe him: no one could be more scrupulously courteous about correspondence than John. Anyway, I was in no way deterred from sending him Home when David Storey delivered his play to the Royal Court.

Looking back I realise that asking John to play in Home was an inspiration — not a calculation. David had specified two leading men in their late forties. But I felt that Home would only be understood and recognised if it was performed by actors of the greatest skill and stature. 'Let's try John Gielgud,' I said: and so we did. I shall never forget the smile, equally delighted and amazed, on the face of Gillian Diamond, when she strode into the director's office the next day. 'Gielgud wants to do it! His agent says he loves the play. He thinks it's terribly funny....'

John took it, just like that. He was by now completely transformed from the careful conservative who had advised Ralph Richardson not to do Waiting for Godot. In fact it was he who suggested Ralph Richardson. 'But do you think he will want to be directed?' I asked apprehensively. 'Oh yes,' John replied. 'He loves direction. As long as he can respect it.' Well, Ralph and I had a big drink and a convivial chat, and he agreed to do it. So did Dandy and Mona. And so began one of those uniquely happy, harmonious and fulfilling theatre experiences that happen, if one is lucky, once in a lifetime. The kind that forge friendships which last the rest of one's life.

We started with an extra week (beyond the statutory four) with John and Ralph alone on the Royal Court stage. We were joined by David Storey and we had a marvellous time, exploring the long duologue, apparently so inconsequential but profoundly revealing, comic yet suggestive, with which the play begins. No working method could have been freer, more sensitive or imaginative than John's and Ralph's. Ralph would discuss perceptively with David, I would contribute on a more superficial level of theatrical effectiveness — and John would listen, suggest, and wait for the cuts. He did not mark these, as most of us do, with pencil or crayon: he would call for a pair of scissors and cut them out. So that by the end of the week his script was in shreds and had to be reprinted. With rare wisdom — sometimes perhaps even rashly — John never seemed to mind losing a line. If anything, he is too respectful of his collaborators, too trusting. In the case of David Storey, of course, his respect was justified: his gracious confidence was lovely to see.

I remember an early run-through of Home. I was sitting in the Circle. John made his entrance, looked round, appreciated the day, sat down and crossed his legs. He noticed a piece of fluff on his trousers. Carefully he removed it. I caught my breath. I wish I could convey the absolute reality — and at the same time the supreme, musical elegance of that action. I am sure he had done it before in rehearsal: but this was a run-through, and John had suddenly begun to act, or found himself acting. The result was an intensity, a size, that created art out of nothing. I looked down at my script: the direction was there. I had never particularly noticed it.

It is hard to express the sheer and absolute actor's genius of John Gielgud. Not his lyrical voice and perfection of phrasing — which became a trap of which he was very well aware. Not his great, inherited actor's intelligence (not intellect — John himself is always amused at the thought that he has been considered an intellectual actor. Intellectual actors are almost always bad actors). John Gielgud is an actor of instinct, sensibility, emotion. His rhetoric is impeccable; but his moments of pure, exposed emotion are inexpressibly touching. In this, for me, lies the unique poetry of his playing.

LINDSAY ANDERSON

HOME – 1970

Ralph Richardson as Jack and John Gielgud as Harry in David Storey's Home, *directed by Lindsay Anderson at the Royal Court Theatre. The production transferred to the Apollo Theatre and then to the Morosco Theatre, New York.*

WHEN LINDSAY ANDERSON offered Gielgud and Richardson *Home*, they could not decide which role they wanted to play. Richardson offered to play Jack because Jack did conjuring tricks and he could conjure.

The home of the title was not, as an audience might have presumed, an old people's home, but a mental institution. There was no story, no action, just two old men chatting away about nothing in particular, the line between fact and fantasy constantly blurred. The dialogue could not have been more trivial, more common-place. The play went on between the lines, in the silences.

There was very little communication, everything was implied, nothing stated. Sentences were left hanging in the air. At times it seemed as if all Gielgud was saying was 'Oh, dear,' 'Oh, yes,' and 'Oh, no.' (The actors thought they would go out of their minds trying to remember their cues; they were all the same.) Some audiences were so convinced by what they saw and heard, they thought the actors, rather than the characters they were playing, were gaga.

Home was a wonderful vehicle for Gielgud and Richardson, who made beautiful music from David Storey's fragmented score. Their sensitive and subtle performances were so totally interdependent that the *Evening Standard*, when it came to make its annual drama awards, rightly gave them a joint award for best actor.

IN GOOD KING CHARLES'S GOLDEN DAYS – 1970

John Gielgud as Charles II in Bernard Shaw's In Good King Charles's Golden Days, *directed by Basil Coleman for BBC Television.*

IN GOOD KING CHARLES'S GOLDEN DAYS, written when Shaw was in his seventies, and described by him as 'a true history that never happened', is rarely performed; and understandably so.

A lot of well-known actors sat around in costume pretending to be Charles II, Nell Gwyn, Isaac Newton, George Fox, the Duchess of Cleveland, James II, the Duchess of Portsmouth, and they just talked. It could not have been more boring. The historical characters were mere mouthpieces.

The best moment, in a plodding production, came right at the end, when the *conversazione* stopped for a domestic scene between the King and Catherine of Braganza, touchingly played by Elisabeth Bergner.

CAESAR AND CLEOPATRA – 1971

Anna Calder-Marshall as Cleopatra and John Gielgud as Caesar in Bernard Shaw's Caesar and Cleopatra, *directed by Robin Phillips at the Chichester Festival Theatre.*

CAESAR AND CLEOPATRA is an empty and silly trifle, surprisingly short on intellect and good lines. Robin Phillips decided to camp it all up with a determinedly larky modern production of a kind with which the RSC had made audiences over-familiar. He set the action in an all-white nursery, with rocking-horse, water-chutes and beach balls (on which the actors bounced up and down). All this may have emphasised the young queen's childishness, but it certainly didn't do much for Egypt.

Gielgud, gentle yet authoritative, was persuasive as Caesar but the role does not offer the actor anything like the opportunities Cleopatra does the actress.

HASSAN – 1971

John Gielgud as the Caliph, Milton Reid as Masrur and William Lyon Brown as Jafar in James Elroy Flecker's Hassan, *directed by Rex Tucker for BBC Television.*

HASSAN, with its perfumed prose, is *Arabian Nights* kitsch, written by an author who has seen *Les Ballets Russes* in *Scheherazade* and never got over it. Ralph Richardson played Hassan.

I first met John Gielgud years ago when I was seventeen. He was in Measure for Measure at Stratford. I saw the matinée and went back afterwards to his dressing-room where he gave me a cup of tea and a biscuit. Val Gielgud, his brother, was there. My father had been stage director for his tour of the Middle and Far East in 1945 and had been in the prompt corner the last time he played Hamlet in Cairo.
When I met him again it was on a hillside in Turkey; a large proportion of the Turkish Army was preparing to go up a much larger hill dressed as Coldstream Guardsmen and Highlanders and British Infantry of the Line for Tony Richardson. He said quite warmly, 'Ah, you're Jolly Jack Wood's son!' I suppose I am. Until we came back to England I didn't miss one scene of Gielgud's. I already felt that I knew him, so much so that I once made the remark that his Hamlet was the finest of his generation with such authority an older actor snapped: 'How do you know? You weren't born.' Well, I had heard about it a lot, from my father I suppose.
Later on I wrote Veterans, *a play inspired by that period in Turkey, the long waits in the sun, the weekend picnics, distinguished old actors dressed as Victorian generals waiting to perform. When I had written it I sent it to Gielgud with some trepidation. I had written H in the hope that he would play Havelock. He didn't like the play, called it 'monologues in front of burning cities'. This became the alternative title, it was so apt. To my astonishment I had a letter back from Gielgud after he had read* Veterans, *saying when he would be free! I had never thought he would want to play Sir Geoffrey. When we were casting* Veterans *John Gielgud was consulted about all the other parts. He made a classic Gielgud remark about a particular actress: 'Oh no, she's doing awfully well now, she wouldn't want to do anything that wasn't absolutely first class'. I took his point.*

CHARLES WOOD

HAMLET – 1971

John Gielgud as the Ghost in Shakespeare's Hamlet, *directed by Peter Wood for ATV.*

T HE PLAY was updated to the nineteenth century. Richard Chamberlain's Hamlet was in the romantic mould, a Regency buck, while Gielgud, in his Napoleonic cape and tricorned hat, a ghostly figure in grey, looked as if he had been hewn out of alabaster.

The commercial television channel, mindful of its mass audience, cut the play to 105 minutes.

What we had, in fact, was not the play without the prince, but very nearly the prince without the play.
BARRY NORMAN *THE TIMES*

VETERANS – 1972

John Gielgud as Sir Geoffrey Kendle and Bob Hoskins as Bernie the Volt in Charles Wood's Veterans, *directed by Ronald Eyre at the Royal Court Theatre.*

W HEN *Veterans* was on its pre-London tour audiences were deeply shocked by the bad language. 'Don't use that word again in front of my wife!' said one particularly irate man at Brighton's Theatre Royal.

Gielgud received a number of rude letters, telling him that he had degraded the profession; one woman even went so far as to enclose a postal order for 40p, with a note to the effect that she presumed he must be very hard up to be appearing in such a play.

Veterans, a satire on films and filming, which clearly had come out of Charles Wood's experiences while making *The Charge of the Light Brigade* in Turkey, was essentially an in-joke at Gielgud's expense. He played a gossiping actor-knight who gets his own way by seeming to be very sweet, very innocent and enormously charming.

Gielgud gave a brilliant parody of himself. The funniest scene was the one he shared with Bob Hoskins, where the crudity of an over-familiar cockney lighting-man was hilariously juxtaposed with the absent-minded politeness of the actor.

There was also a memorable first act curtain when he was left stranded, sitting astride a wobbly wooden prop horse, all alone, not having the faintest idea what he was meant to be doing, and then, on the off-stage cry of 'Action!', mouthing a speech that had been cut and which, through the gunfire and smoke, could hardly be heard anyway.

LOST HORIZON – 1973

Peter Finch as Richard Conway and John Gielgud as Chang in the musical film version of James Hilton's Lost Horizon, *directed by Charles Jarrott.*

THE ROLE OF CHANG, the Oxford-educated spokesman for the two-hundred-year-old High Lama of Shangri-La, was to have been played by Toshiro Mifune, until it was discovered he couldn't speak English.

DELIVER US FROM EVIL – 1973

John Gielgud as Frederick William Densham in Hugh Whitemore's Deliver Us From Evil, *directed by David Sullivan Proudfoot for BBC Television.*

GIELGUD was cast as the demented rector of a small Cornish community, who is so obsessed with saving the innocent from evil that he keeps them prisoner in his derelict house.

11 HARROWHOUSE – 1974

Jack Watson as Miller, John Gielgud as Meecham, Peter Vaughan as Coglin, Jack Watling as Fitzmaurice and, on the floor, James Mason as Watts in 11 Harrowhouse, *a film directed by Aram Avakian.*

11 HARROWHOUSE was a facetious comedy-thriller about a robbery of 12 billion-dollars-worth of uncut diamonds from an impregnable vault.

Gielgud, cast as a totally ruthless controller of the world's trade in diamonds, played him with glacial urbanity.

GALILEO – 1974

Topol as Galileo and John Gielgud as the Old Cardinal in the film version of Bertolt Brecht's Galileo, *directed by Joseph Losey.*

THE OLD CARDINAL is not at all pleased to learn that the earth is not the centre of the universe.

MURDER ON THE ORIENT EXPRESS – 1974

Anthony Perkins as Hector McQueen, Richard Widmark as Ratchett and John Gielgud as Beddoes in the film version of Agatha Christie's Murder on the Orient Express, *directed by Sydney Lumet.*

Murder on the Orient Express, a classic 1930s detective story, has one of Agatha Christie's most celebrated denouements, when it is discovered *everybody* did it. Since the solution is all and the characters and action nil, the production put its trust in the star-system (a star in every role) and the period fashion, the Art Deco designs being handsomely realised by Tony Walton. The film's success at the box office led to an unending Christie revival on big and small screen alike.

Gielgud played the valet to the murdered man. Albert Finney was Hercule Poirot.

GOLD – 1974

Bradford Dillman as Manfred Steyner and John Gielgud as Farrell in Gold, *a film directed by Peter Hunt.*

GIELGUD was cast as the head of an international syndicate who plans to flood a South African mine in order to raise the price of gold in the world market.

John Gielgud, the most vicious tycoon, does most of the talking and all of the acting.
MARGARET HINXMAN *DAILY MAIL*

FRANKENSTEIN: THE TRUE STORY – 1974

Nicola Pagett as Elizabeth Fanshawe and John Gielgud as the Chief Constable in Frankenstein: The True Story, *directed by Jack Smight for television and later dismantled and recut for the big screen.*

THE CREATURE, played by Michael Sarrazin, was so beautiful that Frankenstein fell in love with him.

THE TEMPEST – 1974

Michael Feast as Ariel and John Gielgud as Prospero in Shakespeare's The Tempest, *directed by Peter Hall for the National Theatre, at the Old Vic Theatre.*

BINGO – 1974

John Gielgud as Shakespeare in Edward Bond's Bingo, *directed by Jane Howell and John Dove at the Royal Court Theatre.*

Peter Hall's operatic production, a fine piece of Baroque theatre, gave the Masque element its right and proper place, concentrating on scenic effects and out Inigo-ing Jones. The critics were divided between those who thought it was fabulous and those who thought it was dreadful.

Gielgud (dressed to look like Dr Dee, the Elizabethan astrologer) had a wonderful reception on the first night, which many felt was for the theatrical pleasure he had given in the past rather than for his present performance. There was surprisingly little vocal magic. The major set-pieces could all be heard much better in his recording of *Ages of Man*.

Bingo, a didactic piece of unrelieved violence and misery, described Shakespeare's last years at Stratford-upon-Avon. The great man, disillusioned, worn-out and dying, brooded on the emptiness of his life and the irony that everybody (barring himself and his family) should find him serene and humane. 'There is no limit to my hatred', he confessed. 'It cannot be satisfied with cruelty.'

Gielgud was totally believable as the author of Shakespeare's plays; and indeed, with his high dome, he looked as if he might well have sat for the portrait that appeared on the title page of the first folio. However, for far too much of the time, he merely had to suffer in silence, stupefied with all the suffering he had seen, and Arthur Lowe, with just one scene, as a very drunk Ben Jonson on the cadge, walked off with the play.

John Gielgud graced my play No Man's Land *in 1975. I was honoured. He has been, and remains, an inspiration.*

HAROLD PINTER

NO MAN'S LAND – 1975

Michael Feast as Foster, Ralph Richardson as Hirst, Terence Rigby as Briggs and John Gielgud as Spooner in Harold Pinter's No Man's Land, *directed by Peter Hall for the National Theatre, at the Old Vic Theatre. The production transferred to Longacre Theatre, New York, in 1976.*

You are in no man's land. Which never moves, which never changes, which never grows older, but which remains forever, icy and silent.

N o Man's Land was an enigmatic game, batted and fielded by two elderly literary gents, in elegant oval surroundings, with characteristic Pinteresque wit and menace.

Gielgud, with his crumpled grey pin-stripe suit, his even more crumpled Auden-like face, his gold-rimmed spectacles, sandalled feet, dishevelled lank mousey hair, and bulging tummy, was totally unrecognizable – a memorable physical transformation, quite unlike anything he had attempted before.

Spooner is a creep: a small-time poet, who has fallen on hard times, doomed to yet another failure when he tries to ingratiate himself with his rich and famous host, finally begging for a post as his secretary. The vulnerability, beneath the surface pride and arrogance, was brilliantly caught in a long and very funny speech in which he recites his *curriculum vitae*, listing a whole variety of skills.

No Man's Land, tantalising, elusive, theatrically riveting, offered Gielgud and Richardson two of their finest modern parts.

EDWARD THE SEVENTH – 1975

*John Gielgud as Benjamin Disraeli and Annette Crosbie as
Queen Victoria in a television adaptation of Sir Philip Magnus's
Edward the Seventh, directed by John Gorrie for ATV.
Timothy West played Edward.*

ACES HIGH – 1976

John Gielgud as the Headmaster and Malcolm McDowell as John Gresham in Aces High, *a film directed by Jack Gold.*

ACES HIGH, a remake of *Journey's End*, took R.C. Sheriff's First World War play out of the trenches and into the skies for some brilliantly orchestrated air battles. The public schoolboys were now fighting for God, King and Country in the elite Royal Flying Corps, their average life-span, as pilots, in 1917, being less than a fortnight.

Gielgud made a brief appearance in the opening sequence at Eton, leading morning prayers in chapel, with some fatuous patriotic waffle about 'playing the game for the game's sake'. The man was clearly a first cousin to the headmaster in *40 Years On*.

THE PICTURE OF DORIAN GRAY – 1976

John Gielgud as Lord Henry Wotton and Peter Firth as Dorian Gray in Oscar Wilde's The Picture of Dorian Gray, *directed by John Gorrie for BBC Television.*

The only way to get rid of temptation is to yield to it.

WILDE's *fin de siècle* decadence, a fashionable mixture of self-indulgent homosexuality and epigram, was given a high polish.

THE GRAND INQUISITOR – 1977

John Gielgud as the Grand Inquisitor in Fydor Dostoyevsky's The Grand Inquisitor, *directed by Richard Argent for the Open University – BBC Television.*

JULIUS CAESAR – 1977

Brian Cox as Brutus, John Gill as Popilius Lena, Peter Carlisle as Publius, Gawn Granger as Casca, John Gielgud as Caesar, Martin Friend as Cicero, Pitt Wilkinson as Cinna and Norman Claridge as Caius Ligarius in Shakespeare's Julius Caesar, *directed by John Schlesinger at the National Theatre.*

WITH GIELGUD cast in the title role and his face everywhere in enormous effigies and huge photographic blow-ups, there never was any doubt, from the moment the audience entered the Olivier auditorium, that Caesar was going to be the hero of the play. Even his ghost appeared in triplicate at Philippi.

Vocally, too, he dominated a lifeless production, most critics came to bury. There was, in fact, so little urgency, that it was not clear why Caesar, admittedly insolent and arrogant, but not particularly tyrannical, needed to be assassinated.

Michael Billington, writing in the *Guardian*, wittily dismissed the conspiracy as 'a gratuitous attempt to kill off the best verse-speaker on the English stage'.

VOLPONE – 1977

John Gielgud as Sir Politic Wouldbe and Ian Charleson as Peregrine in Ben Jonson's Volpone, *directed by Peter Hall at the National Theatre.*

SIR POLITIC Wouldbe is a joke at the expense of the gullible English abroad. A Jacobean audience might well have been amused at the sight of an eccentric and stupid man disguising himself as a giant tortoise in order to avoid arrest; but there was nothing funny about watching Gielgud scampering about the stage on all fours. The actor was far more degraded than Sir Politic.

HALF-LIFE – 1977

Avril Elgar as Helen Mallock, Richard Pearson as Francis Mallock, Oliver Cotton as Mike Clayton, Isabel Dean as Barbara Burney, John Gielgud as Sir Noel Cunliffe and Hugh Paddick as Rupert Carter in Julian Mitchell's Half-Life, directed by Waris Hussein at the National Theatre. The production transferred to the Duke of York's Theatre in 1978.

SIR NOEL CUNLIFFE, an arrogant and rich professor of archeology, finds that his whole life, professionally and emotionally, has been built on a false premise and is determined that the university shall not have one penny of his fortune when he dies.

Half-Life, a civilised, acid-witty West End play, offered Gielgud splendid opportunities to be devastatingly rude; and it was a real pleasure listening to him putting the boot in to his colleagues and so-called friends.

John Gielgud, as Cunliffe, spits and hisses insults like a self-satisfied snake enchanted with the sound of its own rattle. When, for a moment, his past looms up like an awful lie his temporary loss of composure is most moving.
MILTON SHULMAN *EVENING STANDARD*

PROVIDENCE – 1977

John Gielgud as Clive Langham and Peter Arne as Nils in
Providence, *a film directed by Alain Resnais.*

CLIVE is a randy, roaring, drunken, foul-mouthed, incontinent, seventy-eight-year-old novelist, refusing to go gently into the night: 'You won't get me, you fucking bastards!'

Drinking bottle after bottle of chilled Chablis, while slipping pessaries up his backside, he plots his new novel.

Providence, perhaps Resnais's best film since *L'An-née dernière à Marienbad*, is about the creative process itself, the imagination hard at work, constantly interrupted by nightmares and memories, the line of demarcation between what is fantasy and what is reality deliberately blurred.

Gielgud, as Clive, relishing the scatological abuse, the self-disgust, and even the pain, had one of his great screen roles. The reconciliation scene with his real family (so different from the imagined family in his novel) was beautifully judged and the actual moment of farewell – 'Just leave . . . Now please . . . Neither kiss nor touch . . . With my blessing . . .' – was deeply touching.

This must be John Gielgud's finest, most sustained film performance – an elegantly ferocious gauge against which others must be compared in the future. We have heard the rapier-swish before, but rarely the sledgehammer-smash. This is acting with guts as well as mind.
TOM HUTCHINSON *SUNDAY TELEGRAPH*

At the centre of it all Gielgud's performance is so realistically painful that it is sometimes almost unbearable to watch.
FELIX BARKER *EVENING NEWS*

HEARTBREAK HOUSE – 1977

John Gielgud as Captain Shotover and Lesley-Anne Down as Ellie Dunn in Bernard Shaw's Heartbreak House, *directed by Cedric Messina for BBC Television.*

Shaw described his comedy as a fantasia in the Russian manner; but his characters are not real enough for the comparison to hold.

Gielgud would not be many people's first choice for Shotover, a Conradian sailor, who, having sold his soul to the devil and married a West Indian negress, is now working on an invention to blow up the human race.

John Gielgud was not endowed by nature to be everyone's idea of a bluff old sea-dog. The many glasses of rum he was supposed to have pushed back during the day, much to the author's disapproval, would more plausibly have been a dry sherry or two.
PHILIP PURSER *SUNDAY TELEGRAPH*

LES MISÉRABLES – 1978

Christopher Guard as Marius and John Gielgud as Gillenormand in Victor Hugo's Les Misérables, *directed for television by Glenn Jordan. Richard Jordan played Jean Valjean and Anthony Perkins played Inspector Javert.*

ROMEO AND JULIET – 1978

John Gielgud as Chorus in Shakespeare's Romeo and Juliet, *directed by Alvin Rakoff for BBC Television.*

NO MAN'S LAND – 1978

Ralph Richardson as Hirst and John Gielgud as Spooner in the Peter Hall National Theatre production of Harold Pinter's No Man's Land, *directed by Julian Amyes for Granada Television.*

T HE DISADVANTAGE of getting Gielgud to speak the prologue, all fourteen lines of it, is that it is unfair on the other actors who then have to do the play.

Hywel Bennett and Kika Markham were the star-cross'd lovers.

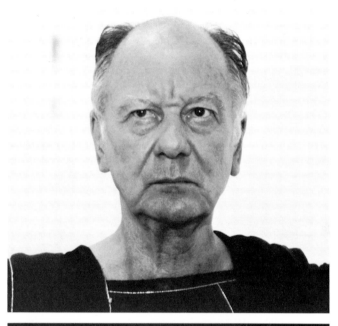

RICHARD II – 1978

John Gielgud as John of Gaunt and Derek Jacobi as Richard in Shakespeare's Richard II, *directed by David Giles for BBC Television.*

Gielgud as John of Gaunt looked, as P.G. Wodehouse would have remarked, like a burst horsechair sofa.
RICHARD LAST *DAILY TELEGRAPH*

CALIGULA – 1979

John Gielgud as Nerva in the film version of Gore Vidal's Caligula, *directed by Tinto Brass, Giancarlo Lui, Bob Guccione and Franco Rossellini.**

GIELGUD originally turned down the part of Tiberius, saying the film was 'pure pornography'. But when Gore Vidal wrote him a letter, saying how impertinent it was of him to refuse the part and that if he knew what Tennessee Williams and Edward Albee were saying about him, he would not be so grand, he, somewhat shamefacedly, accepted the smaller role of the Senecan tutor and adviser to Tiberius, now played by Peter O'Toole. Nerva dies early on, having slit his wrists in the bath.

Caligula, at 17 million dollars, was the most expensive hard porn flick ever made: two and a half hours of sex, sadism, murder, castrations, beheadings, a cavalcade of genitalia in huge close-up. The extras, taking part in the orgy scenes, hadn't had such a good time since the silent movie days of Cecil B. de Mille.

When Gore Vidal saw the final film, he sued for his name to be removed from the credit titles.

* *Nobody was actually credited with directing the film. When Tinto Brass was fired, Lui, Guccione and Rossellini completed it.*

NECK – 1979

John Gielgud as Jelks and Joan Collins as Lady Turton in Roald Dahl's Neck, *a tale of the unexpected, directed by Christopher Miles for Anglia Television.*

JOAN COLLINS was cast as the faithless wife of a newspaper tycoon. She lost her head – decapitated by her husband, with the assistance of his butler and some modern sculpture. Gielgud played the butler.

A PORTRAIT OF THE ARTIST AS A YOUNG MAN – 1979

John Gielgud as the Preacher in the film version of James Joyce's A Portrait of the Artist as a Young Man, *directed by Joseph Strick.*

Oₙₑ of the most memorable moments in the novel is the preacher's vivid sermon on damnation and the torments of hell.

He speaks the words well enough, his precise diction giving them something like the burning power of dry ice. But in the truncated form the screen demands, they lose much of their power.

TIME

MURDER BY DECREE – 1979

John Gielgud as the Prime Minister, Lord Salisbury, in Murder by Decree, *a film directed by Bob Clark.*

Mᵤₙₐₑₙ ᵦᵧ Dₑ꜀ₙₑₑ had Sherlock Holmes (Christopher Plummer) and Dr Watson (James Mason) on the trail of Jack the Ripper in a very foggy and very studio-bound London.

Gielgud appeared right at the end of the film, in an unsatisfactorily staged denouement, in a private courtroom, in which Holmes learns that there is no Jack the Ripper and that he is the invention of the government, whose agents are murdering the prostitutes, as part of a royal cover-up to protect the Duke of Clarence.

1980s

John Gielgud as Hobson in Arthur *1981.*

THE HUMAN FACTOR – 1980

John Gielgud as Brigadier Tomlinson and Richard Attenborough as Colonel John Daintry in the film version of Graham Greene's The Human Factor, *directed by Otto Preminger.*

GIELGUD made a very brief appearance as a senior security officer.

WHY DIDN'T THEY ASK EVANS? – 1980

John Gielgud as the Rev Thomas Jones and Francesca Annis as Lady Frances Derwent in Agatha Christie's Why Didn't They Ask Evans?, *directed by John Davies and Tony Wharmby for LWT.*

WHY DIDN'T THEY ASK EVANS? (which starred Agatha Christie's two amateur detectives) had obviously been conceived as a serial; but somebody had second thoughts and it was presented in one long and boring three-and-a-half hour sitting. The hats were far and away more interesting than the murder mystery.

THE ELEPHANT MAN – 1980

Nula Conwell as Nurse Kathleen, John Gielgud as Carr Gomm and Anthony Hopkins as Frederick Treves in The Elephant Man, *a film directed by David Lynch.*

THE ELEPHANT MAN (played by John Hurt) was John Merrick, so obscenely deformed that he could earn his living only as a freak in a circus.

The film, quite different to the play, purported to be the true story; though certain scenes were so sensational, and so atmospherically shot, as to be straight out of a Victorian penny dreadful.

Carr Gomm was the administrator of the London Hospital who bends the rules so that Merrick may be admitted.

THE ENGLISH GARDEN – 1980

John Gielgud as the presenter of The English Garden, *a seven-part history of the English garden through the ages, directed by Richard Mervyn for Thames Television. He is seen here in the gardens of Stourhead.*

PARSON'S PLEASURE – 1980

Bernard Miles as Mr Rummins and John Gielgud as Cyril Boggis in Roald Dahl's Parson's Pleasure, *a tale of the unexpected, directed by John Bruce for Anglia Television.*

CYRIL BOGGIS is a rogue antique dealer, masquerading as a clergyman. He is so successful in convincing a farmer that a priceless Chippendale commode is worthless that the farmer saws the legs off it before he can take it away.

SPHINX – 1981

John Gielgud as Abdu Hamdi and Lesley-Anne Down as Erica Baron in Sphinx, *a film directed by Franklin J. Shaffner.*

THE CRITICS were in total agreement about *Sphinx*, one of those Curse-of-Tutankhamun thrillers, with splendid views of Luxor and Saqqara. It sphinx, they said.

Gielgud was cast as a Cairo antique dealer and black-marketeer who gets brutally murdered early on. Margaret Hinxman, writing in the *Daily Mail*, thought he looked like a coffee-coloured Old Mother Riley in his djellaba and skull cap.

THE SEVEN DIALS MYSTERY – 1981

John Gielgud as the Marquis of Caterham and Christopher Scoular as Bill Evers Leigh in Agatha Christie's The Seven Dials Mystery, *directed by Tony Wharmby for LWT.*

THE SEVEN DIALS MYSTERY, a mediocre Christie thriller, was really just another excuse for more cloche hats, vintage cars and beautiful scenery.

OMAR MUKHTAR – LION OF THE DESERT – 1981

John Gielgud as Sharif El-Gariani and Anthony Quinn as Omar Mukhtar in Omar Mukhtar – Lion of the Desert, *a film directed by Moustapha Akkad.*

OMAR MUKHTAR was the Bedouin guerilla who fought against Mussolini's army in Libya in the 1920s and 1930s. He was finally captured and hanged.

Sheikh Gariani was an Arab who decided it would be more expedient to collaborate with the Italians. Gielgud was barely recognisable behind his enormous white beard.

I, like many other people, have seen Sir John on stage – in such wildly diverse creations as The Tempest, and Alan Bennett's 40 Years On. I remember, when I saw him in 40 Years On, that I thought his aptitude for comedy was delicious. He seemed almost to act in the same way as he did in classical roles ... with the same passion – which, in comic situations, became comic without it seeming to be an extra effort on his part. When Arthur was being put together, I felt that Sir John would be ideal for the role, rather than other actors who would probably overlay the part with a veneer of glucose. I think I can safely say that I was right in that assessment. Of course the world loved him in that film and he won the Oscar for his supporting role. There was a no-nonsense approach during the filming which pleased me no end. I'm not one for discussion too much when it comes to acting. I felt it would be fun just to do it, to rehearse on camera as it were. It seemed that we didn't have to alter our performances any, once we had done the first takes. When we had a technical problem, which we did now and again, he was almost indefatigable being patient and aware of the difficulties one encounters in movie-making. Perhaps if I'd been a young actor with him at the time, for instance when he was directing Alec Guinness, I might have had a rather more tangled experience of him. Recently, I have been reading the memoirs of Alec Guinness, who felt very dashed, I think, at some point, by Sir John's vigorous criticism of everyone on stage. Perhaps this attitude has mellowed over the years – or perhaps when he's not directing he does not have the same feeling about the work he does in that situation ... obviously having a little less control.

I found him a charming man ... delightful and of course wonderfully reliable to work with. He brought a sense of humanity to the part of Hobson in Arthur, which, coupled with his wonderful sense of the acerbic and priggish in that character, made for a very full and rounded performance. I liked most of all I think, for my own part, the moment when he is in hospital and I am looking after him. He says 'Arthur, you're a good son'. It broke my heart to hear that and I remember being very moved on the set. Whenever I see that scene, I am moved. That moment expresses all the longings that we all had for approval from a gentle father. In that moment he provided that consoling embrace.

The poetry that's in this man will sustain him and nurture his spirit. We all need that poetry in one way or another. He has found his.

DUDLEY MOORE

ARTHUR – 1981

Dudley Moore as Arthur Bach and John Gielgud as Hobson in
Arthur, *a film directed by Steve Gordon.*

Arthur: I think I'll take a bath.
Hobson: I'll alert the media.

Aʀᴛʜᴜʀ was a playboy millionaire, a cute and amiable drunk, who hadn't grown up, and the nicest thing about the film (a screwball comedy in the 1930s manner) was the father/son relationship between him and his valet, Hobson, the perfect gentleman's gentleman, in everything but vocabulary. There was a beautifully written death scene, impeccably played by both actors, which was genuinely moving.

Gielgud, who had turned the script down twice because of the bad language and because he didn't want to play what he thought was going to be a conventional Jeeves part, scored one of his biggest screen successes. And it was, of course, the marriage of posh English accent and foul-mouthed obscenities ('Perhaps you'd like me to come in there and wash your dick, you little shit?') which proved so irresistible to audiences, for whom there was the additional comic *frisson* that it was Sir John Gielgud, the distinguished Shakespearian actor and knight, who was saying such things.

The British critics were notably cooler than their American counterparts, many thinking that the film would not do Gielgud's reputation any good at all; whereas, in fact, *Arthur* made Gielgud an international star, winning him an 'Oscar' and the New York and Los Angeles Critics' Awards.

CHARIOTS OF FIRE – 1981

John Gielgud as the Provost of Trinity and Lindsay Anderson as the Master of Caius in Chariots of Fire, *a film directed by Hugh Hudson.*

Chariots of Fire celebrated the 1924 Olympic champions, Harold Abrahams and Eric Liddell, their two separate stories running in tandem. The film, relying heavily on slow-motion and theme music, managed to be wildly patriotic while at the same time knocking the Establishment. It was an Oscar-winning combination.

Gielgud and Anderson were cast as fictional figures: two obnoxious hypocrites, condescending, bigoted and racially prejudiced, who are put in their place by Abrahams.

BRIDESHEAD REVISITED – 1981

Jeremy Irons as Charles Ryder and John Gielgud as Edward Ryder in Evelyn Waugh's Brideshead Revisited, *directed by Charles Sturridge and Michael Lindsay-Hogg for Granada Television.*

The dinner-table was our battlefield.

THE SCENES at the dinner-table, between Charles and his father, were among the most enjoyable and memorable in the serial. There was that moment, for instance, when Ryder père asks after Sebastian, knowing full-well that he has never been ill:

'That friend you were so much concerned about, did he die?'

'No.'

'I am very thankful. You should have written to tell me. I worried about him so much.'

The hypocrisy, the sheer nastiness of that last sentence, was so perfectly phrased that it is impossible to read it now without hearing Gielgud's voice.

The man's meanness, his petulance, his malice, the delight he takes in his son's impecuniosity and discomfort, all were played for brilliant high comedy.

John Gielgud played Mr Ryder as if he had been doing it all his life. Perhaps he has: aloof and yet alert, calculating but dismissive; he seemed to have sprung on to the screen from the pages without pausing to alter that wry, malevolent expression.

PETER ACKROYD *TIMES EDUCATIONAL SUPPLEMENT*

DYRYGENT – 1981

Krystyna Janda as Marta and John Gielgud as Jan Lasocki in
Dyrygent, *a film directed by Andrzej Wajda.*
English title: The Conductor.

DYRYGENT, which was produced before Gdánsk, was an allegory of freedom and a satire on the way central government manipulates culture for political ends.

Jan Lasocki was an elderly Polish émigré conductor who returns home for the first time in fifty years to conduct his small town's orchestra in Beethoven's *Fifth Symphony*.

Before he began filming, Gielgud took a four-day crash-course in conducting. 'The instrumentalists reward me', he wrote at the time, 'by tapping their music stands when I manage to sustain correctly a few bars and smile sympathetically when I make mistakes.'

Gielgud had no difficulty in conveying a great man, capable of inspiring affection and restoring self-confidence and unity; but he was hampered by some appalling dubbing (which gave him quite the wrong Polish voice) and a death scene, in a queue of people waiting to hear his concert, which had not been properly thought through.

If any orchestra followed Gielgud's inflexible beat the result would be certain cacophany.
GEOFF BROWN *TIMES*

INSIDE THE THIRD REICH – 1982

John Gielgud as Albert Speer Snr in Inside The Third Reich, *a film for television, directed by Marvin J. Chomsky.*

INSIDE THE THIRD REICH was based on the best-selling memoirs of Albert Speer, Hitler's architect, the second most powerful man in Nazi Germany, a consummate Faust-like opportunist whose grandiose designs were firmly rooted in Fascist fantasies.

Gielgud is haughtily endearing, a stiff-collared gentleman who speaks in the cadences of Schiller and dreams in the images of Goethe.
RICHARD CORLISS *TIME*

SCANDALOUS – 1982

John Gielgud as Uncle Willie in Scandalous, *a film directed by Rob Cohen.*

UNCLE WILLIE is a con man. Gielgud is seen here in one of his many disguises.

THE SCARLET AND THE BLACK – 1983

John Gielgud as Pope Pius XII in The Scarlet and the Black, *a film directed by Jerry London.*

THE FILM was based on the true story of the Irish-born priest, Monsignor Hugh O'Flaherty – the Scarlet Pimpernel of the Vatican – who saved the lives of thousands of allied soldiers and civilians. The role was taken by Gregory Peck.

Pope Pius XII was the Pope who failed to speak out against the extermination of the Jews during the Second World War.

John Gielgud looked as if he were born to be The Pope.
HILARY DORLING *SUNDAY EXPRESS*

THE WICKED LADY – 1983

Faye Dunaway as Lady Skelton and John Gielgud as Hogarth in The Wicked Lady, *a film directed by Michael Winner.*

MICHAEL WINNER managed to whip up a great deal of publicity when the censor threatened to cut a flagellation scene between two semi-naked women, and such distinguished names as Lindsay Anderson, Kingsley Amis, John Mortimer and John Schlesinger, all rushed to his defence.

The Wicked Lady was a bawdy, bosomy burlesque of the old 1945 Margaret Lockwood melodrama, one of the most successful British films ever made, Miss Lockwood's cleavage shocking audiences far more than her wickedness.

Faye Dunaway now played the lady who is so bored with country life that she turns highwaywoman at night. The story was based on fact.

Gielgud was cast as the ancient, God-fearing retainer who discovers her secret and is murdered by her. He described the film as the sort of 'tosherie' his uncle Fred Terry used to take him to see when he was a child.

THE FAR PAVILIONS – 1984

John Gielgud as Major Sir Louis Cavagnari in M.M. Kaye's The Far Pavilions, *directed by Peter Duffell for Channel 4.*

Tнε Far Pavilions, a nineteenth-century forbidden romance between a British cavalry officer and an Indian princess, was a three-part, six-hour, mini-series for those who might have found *The Jewel in the Crown* a bit too up-market for their taste. The story was set during the Second Afghan War and Gielgud is seen here defending the British Mission at Kabal against the Afghan rebels.

There was a spectacular wedding procession and ceremony (involving 1,000 extras, 20 elephants, 120 bullocks and herds of cows, goats and sheep) which lasted very nearly as long as an actual Indian wedding.

SIX CENTURIES OF VERSE – 1984

Ralph Richardson, Peggy Ashcroft and John Gielgud in the grounds of Beckley Park, near Oxford, during the filming of the fifth programme of Six Centuries of Verse, *which was devoted to the work of Shakespeare and directed by Richard Mervyn for Thames Television.*

Thinking of John and all he has contributed to our theatre in the last sixty odd years, what comes uppermost to mind?
I think, firstly, the lasting influence he has had, ever since the thirties, when he formed his companies at the New (now Albery) Theatre and the Queen's. Secondly his generosity and loyalty to all his many loving friends and colleagues. Thirdly the wealth of glorious performances and productions over all these years which he has given us all.
And lastly his exhilarating and inspiring personality, his humility and enormous sense of FUN!
PEGGY ASHCROFT

THE MASTER OF BALLANTRAE – 1984

Michael York as James Durie and John Gielgud as Lord Durrisdeer in Robert Louis Stevenson's The Master of Ballantrae, directed by Douglas Hickox for HTV.

However, if he is going to prostitute his talent by accepting such absurd parts as Lord Durrisdeer he should not give the impression that he is slumming in a smelly neighbourhood or has just swallowed the juice of 11 lemons.

DANIEL FARSON *MAIL ON SUNDAY*

WAGNER – 1985

Ralph Richardson, Laurence Olivier and John Gielgud as three ministers at the court of Ludwig II in Wagner, a film made for television, directed by Tony Palmer. Richard Burton played Wagner.

THE SHOOTING PARTY – 1985

*James Mason as Sir Randolph Nettleby and John Gielgud as
Cornelius Cardew in the film version of Isabel Colegate's*
The Shooting Party, *directed by Alan Bridges.*

THE SHOOTING PARTY (which owed rather too much to
Jean Renoir's *La Règle du Jeu*) was an elegant
Edwardian swansong, the slaughter of birds anticipating
the massacre of men in the First World War.

There wasn't much Gielgud could do with the
diminished role of the eccentric animal rights campaigner, except carry his placard (THOU SHALT NOT
KILL) through the gorse.

He shared a charming little scene with James Mason
(excellent in his last film role) in which Cardew is
disarmed by Nettleby's compliments on the printing of
his pamphlets.

PLENTY – 1985

Meryl Streep as Susan Traherne, John Gielgud as Sir Leonard Darwin and Charles Dance as Raymond Brock in the film version of David Hare's Plenty, *directed by Fred Schepisi.*

DAVID HARE's play traced the spiritual decay of England, and its social decline, in the immediate post-war years. Gielgud was cast as a diplomat of the old school who resigns, at the time of Suez, putting honour before patriotism.

He can make you laugh by an almost imperceptible straightening of his head and neck; his celebrations must be the teeniest any clown has ever mastered. There was an audible happy stir each time he appeared. (When he makes an exit speech, you pity the actors who are left behind, because the energy goes with him.)
PAULINE KAEL *NEW YORKER*

TIME AFTER TIME – 1986

John Gielgud as Jasper Swift in Molly Keane's Time After Time, *directed by Bill Hays for BBC Television.*

JASPER SWIFT and his three sisters, who are the last remaining members of an eccentric and once wealthy Anglo-Irish family, live in a decrepit house in Co. Wicklow. Jasper fancies a young monk.

LEAVE ALL FAIR – 1986

John Gielgud as John Middleton Murry and Jane Birkin as Marie Taylor in Leave All Fair, *a film directed by John Reid.*

LEAVE ALL FAIR is about John Middleton Murry's last visit to France when he is about to publish a book about his wife, Katherine Mansfield.

And I cannot recall when this actor last held the screen with such emotional power. His acting is most refreshingly out of the rut of 'cameo' performances with which he has favoured us so often, or comic roles in which his natural hauteur and disdain can be so funny.
ERIC SHORTER *DAILY TELEGRAPH*

THE THEBAN PLAYS – 1986

John Gielgud as Teiresias in Sophocles' The Theban Plays, *directed by Don Taylor for BBC Television.*

THE THEBAN PLAYS, 2,300 years old, newly translated, and acted in modern costume (Oedipus looked as if he were in an Ivor Novello musical), were spread over three nights.

In *Oedipus the King*, Gielgud's intellectual weight and authority were invaluable. The final accusation – 'You have eyes but you cannot see your corruption. The man you are looking for . . . is here' – was amazingly powerful and as hard as his grip on the king's hand.

In *Antigone*, the make-up department surpassed themselves, making his grim face look even more grotesque and ugly. He was like some magnificent eagle (and just as frightening). His disgust at the stench on his sacrificial altar was vividly expressed.

QUARTERMAINE'S TERMS – 1987

John Gielgud as Eddie Loomis and Edward Fox as St John Quartermaine in Simon Gray's Quartermaine's Terms, *directed by Bill Hays for BBC Television.*

SIMON GRAY's play, a Chekhovian piece, which found a great deal of comedy in other people's tragedies, adapted well to television, with Edward Fox repeating his stage performance of the decent, lonely, incompetent Quartermaine who is constantly used by everybody and then finally ditched.

Gielgud (who had turned down his role in the theatre) played one of the joint principals of a Cambridge School of English for Foreigners, where Quartermaine is meant to be teaching. The comedy – the fussing anxiety and schoolmasterly pep-talks and admonishments – was acted with the gentlest of satiric touches; while the tragedy, of his lover dying, was most movingly understated.

THE CANTERVILLE GHOST – 1987

John Gielgud as Sir Simon de Canterville and Ted Wass as Harry in Oscar Wilde's The Canterville Ghost, *directed by Paul Bogart for HTV.*

WILDE'S GHOST is far wittier in the original – a vain actorish ghost who takes delight in his rich repertoire of impersonations and plans to terrorise his American guests, only to find he is terrorised by them! 'Never in a brilliant and uninterrupted career had he been so grossly insulted.'

What the short story needed was the elegance and irony of a film like *Kind Hearts and Coronets* combined with the fairy tale magic of Jean Cocteau's *La Belle et la Bête.* What it got was an up-dated American production more interested in farce and special effects than style.

Gielgud ('I have not slept for three hundred years, for three hundred years I have not slept, and I am so tired') and fourteen-year-old Alyssa Milano, as the little girl who redeems him, were charming – a quality unbeknown to Wilde's ghost.

THE WHISTLE BLOWER – 1987

John Gielgud as Sir Adrian Chapple and Michael Caine as Frank Jones in The Whistle Blower, *a film directed by Simon Langton.*

GIELGUD played the KGB mole at GCHQ.

CHRONOLOGY

THEATRE

DATE	TITLE	PLAYWRIGHT	ROLE	DIRECTOR	THEATRE
1921/1922 The Old Vic Company at the Old Vic Theatre					
Nov	Henry V	William Shakespeare	Soldier and English Herald	Robert Atkins	
1922					
Mar	Peer Gynt	Henrik Ibsen, translated by William Archer	Walk-on	Robert Atkins	
Mar	King Lear	William Shakespeare	Walk-on	Robert Atkins	
Apr	Wat Tyler	Halcott Glover	Walk-on	Robert Atkins	
Apr	Love is the Best Doctor	Molière	Walk-on	Robert Atkins	
Apr	The Comedy of Errors	William Shakespeare	Walk-on	Robert Atkins	
Apr	As You Like It	William Shakespeare	Walk-on	Robert Atkins	
Oct	The Wheel	J.B. Fagan	Lieutenant Manners	Cecil King	New, Oxford
1925					
Mar	The Masque of Comus	John Milton	Younger Brother	Kathleen Talbot	Middle Temple
May	The Insect Play	Brothers Čapek, freely adapted by Nigel Playfair and Clifford Bax	Felix	Nigel Playfair	Regent
June	Robert E. Lee	John Drinkwater	Aide to General Lee	Nigel Playfair and John Drinkwater	Regent
Dec	Charley's Aunt	Brandon Thomas	Charles Wykeham	Mrs Brandon Thomas	Comedy
1924 The Oxford Players at the Oxford Playhouse					
Jan	Captain Brassbound's Conversion	Bernard Shaw	Johnson	Reginald Denham	
Jan	Love for Love	William Congreve	Valentine	Reginald Denham	
Feb	Mr Pym Passes By	A.A. Milne	Brian Strange	Reginald Denham	
Feb	She Stoops to Conquer	Oliver Goldsmith	Young Marlow	Reginald Denham	
Feb	Monna Vanna	Maurice Maeterlinck, translated by Alfred Sutro	Prinzivalle	J.B. Fagan	
Apr	Romeo and Juliet	William Shakespeare	Paris	Eric Bush	RADA
May	Romeo and Juliet	William Shakespeare	Romeo	H.K. Ayliff	Regent
	The Return Half	John Van Druten	John Sherry	Henzie Raeburn	RADA
The Oxford Players at the Oxford Playhouse					
Oct	Candida	Bernard Shaw	Eugene Marchbanks	J.B. Fagan	
Oct	Deirdre of the Sorrows	John M. Synge	Naisi	J.B. Fagan	
Nov	A Collection Will Be Made	Arthur Eckersley	Paul Roget	J.B. Fagan	
Nov	Everybody's Husband	Gilbert Cannan	A Domino	J.B. Fagan	
Nov	The Cradle Song	Gregorio Martinez Sierra, translated by John Garrett Underhill	Antonio	J.B. Fagan	
Nov	John Gabriel Borkman	Henrik Ibsen, translated by William Archer	Erhart Borkman	J.B. Fagan	
Nov	His Widow's Husband	Jacinto Benavente, translated by John Garrett Underhill	Zurita	J.B. Fagan	
Dec	Madame Pepita	Gregorio Martinez Sierra, translated by John Garrett Underhill	Augusto	J.B. Fagan	
Dec	French Leave	Reginald Berkeley	Lieutenant George Graham	Eric Bush	Charterhouse
1925 The Oxford Players at the Oxford Playhouse					
Jan	A Collection Will Be Made	Arthur Eckersley	Paul Roget	J.B. Fagan	
Jan	Smith	W. Somerset Maugham	Algernon Peppercorn	J.B. Fagan	
Jan	The Cherry Orchard	Anton Chekhov translated by George Calderon	Trofimov	J.B. Fagan	
May	The Orphan	Thomas Otway	Castalio	Allan Wade	Aldwych
Apr	The Nature of the Evidence	Howard Peacey	Ted Hewitt	Guy Pelham Boulton	RADA

DATE	TITLE	PLAYWRIGHT	ROLE	DIRECTOR	THEATRE
May	The Vortex	Noel Coward	Nicky Lancaster	Noel Coward	Little
May	The Cherry Orchard	Anton Chekhov, translated by George Calderon	Trofimov	J.B. Fagan	Lyric, Hammersmith
Jun	The High Constable's Wife	Lewis after Balzac	Julien de Boys-Bourredon	Lewis Casson	Garden

The Oxford Players at the Oxford Playhouse

DATE	TITLE	PLAYWRIGHT	ROLE	DIRECTOR	THEATRE
Aug	The Lady from the Sea	Henrik Ibsen translated by William Archer	A Stranger	J.B. Fagan	
Aug	The Man with a Flower in his Mouth	Luigi Pirandello, translated by Arthur Livingston	The Man	J.B. Fagan	
Sep	The Two Gentlemen of Verona	William Shakespeare	Valentine	Robert Atkins	Apollo
Oct	The Seagull	Anton Chekhov, translated by Constance Garnett	Konstantin	A.E. Filmer	Little
Oct	Dr Faustus	Christopher Marlowe	Good Angel	Allan Wade	New, Oxford
Dec	L'Ecole des Cocottes	Paul Armont and Michel Gerbidon, adapted by H.M. Harwood	Robert	Vere Bennett	Prince's
Dec	Old English Nativity Play		Second Shepherd	Edith Craig	Daly's
1926 Jan	The Tempest	William Shakespeare	Ferdinand	Robert Courtneidge	Savoy
Jan	Sons and Fathers	Allan Monkhouse	Richard Southern	Milton Rosmer	RADA
Feb	Three Sisters	Anton Chekhov, translated by Constance Garnett	Baron Nickolay Tusenbach	Theodore Komisarjevsky	Barnes
Mar	Katerina	Leonid Andreyev, adapted by Herman Bernstein	Georg Stibelev	Theodore Komisarjevsky	Barnes
	Romeo and Juliet (balcony scene)	William Shakespeare	Romeo		Coliseum
Jun	Hamlet	William Shakespeare	Rosencrantz	Barry Jackson	Royal Court
Jul	The Lady of the Camellias	Alexander Dumas fils, adapted by Michael Orme	Armand Duval	Sydney Bland	Garrick
Jul	Confession	W.F. Casey	Wilfred Marlay	Reginald Denham	Royal Court
Sep	The Constant Nymph	Margaret Kennedy and Basil Dean	Lewis Dodd	Basil Dean	New
Dec	Gloriana	Gwen John	Sir John Harrington	George Owen	Little
1927 Apr	Othello	William Shakespeare	Cassio	A.E. Filmer	Apollo
Jun	The Great God Brown	Eugene O'Neill	Dion Anthony	Peter Godfrey	Strand
1928 Jan	The Patriot	Alfred Neumann, adapted by Ashley Dukes	Grand Duke Alexander	Gilbert Miller	Majestic, New York
Mar	Ghosts	Henrik Ibsen, translated by J.T. Grein	Oswald Alving	Peter Godfrey	Wyndhams's
Apr	Ghosts	Henrik Ibsen, translated by J.T. Grein	Oswald Alving	Peter Godfrey	Arts
Jun	Holding Out The Apple	B. Wynne-Bower	Dr Gerald Marloe	Leon M Lion	Globe
Jun	Prejudice	Mercedes de Acosta	Jacob Slovak	Leslie Banks	Arts
Aug	The Skull	Bernard J. McOwen and Harry E. Humphrey	Captain Vernon Allenby	Victor Morley	Shaftesbury
Oct	Fortunato	Serafin and Joaquin Alvarez Quintero. English version by Helen and Harley Granville-Barker	Alberto	James Whale	Royal Court
Oct	The Lady from Alfáqueque	Serafin and Joaquin Alvarez Quintero. English version by Helen and Harley Granville-Barker	Felipe Rivas	James Whale	Royal Court
Nov	Out of the Sea	Don Marquis	John Marstin	Campbell Gullan and Henry Oscar	Strand
1929 Jan	The Seagull	Anton Chekhov, translated by Constance Garnett	Konstantin	A.E. Filmer	Arts
Feb	Red Rust	V.M. Kirchon and A.V.Ouspensky, adapted by Virginia and Frank Vernon	Fédor	Frank Vernon	Little
Mar	Hunter's Moon	Sophus Michaelis, adapted by Harry Graham	Paul de Tressailles	Leslie Faber	Prince of Wales
Apr	The Lady with the Lamp	Reginald Berkeley	Henry Tremayne	Leslie Banks and Edith Evans	Garrick
Apr	Shall We Join the Ladies?	J.M. Barrie	Captain Jennings	Gerald du Maurier	Palace
Jun	Red Sunday	Hubert Griffith	Bronstein (Trotsky)	Theodore Komisarjevsky	Arts

DATE	TITLE	PLAYWRIGHT	ROLE	DIRECTOR	THEATRE

1929 The Old Vic Company at the Old Vic Theatre

DATE	TITLE	PLAYWRIGHT	ROLE	DIRECTOR	THEATRE
Sep	Romeo and Juliet	William Shakespeare	Romeo	Harcourt Williams	
Oct	The Merchant of Venice	William Shakespeare	Antonio	Harcourt Williams	
Oct	The Imaginary Invalid	Molière, freely adapted by F. Anstey	Cléante	Harcourt Williams	
Nov	Richard II	William Shakespeare	Richard	Harcourt Williams	
Dec	Douaumont	Eberhard Wolfgang Moeller. English version by Graham and Tristan Rawson	The Prologue	Peter Godfrey	Prince of Wales

1929/1930 The Old Vic Company at the Old Vic Theatre

DATE	TITLE	PLAYWRIGHT	ROLE	DIRECTOR	THEATRE
Dec	A Midsummer Night's Dream	William Shakespeare	Oberon	Harcourt Williams	
Jan	Julius Caesar	William Shakespeare	Marcus Antonius	Harcourt Williams	
Feb	As You Like It	William Shakespeare	Ferdinand	Harcourt Williams	
Feb	Androcles and the Lion	Bernard Shaw	The Emperor	Harcourt Williams	
Mar	Macbeth	William Shakespeare	Macbeth	Harcourt Williams	
Apr	The Man with a Flower in his Mouth	Luigi Pirandello, translated by Arthur Livingston	The Man	Harcourt Williams	
Apr	The Rehearsal	Maurice Baring	Mr Hughes	Harcourt Williams	
Apr	Hamlet (in its entirety)	William Shakespeare	Hamlet	Harcourt Williams	
Jun	Hamlet	William Shakespeare	Hamlet	Harcourt Williams	Queen's
Jul	The Importance of Being Earnest	Oscar Wilde	John Worthing	Nigel Playfair	Lyric, Hammersmith

1930 The Old Vic Company at the Old Vic Theatre

DATE	TITLE	PLAYWRIGHT	ROLE	DIRECTOR	THEATRE
Sep	Henry IV Part I	William Shakespeare	Hotspur	Harcourt Williams	
Oct	The Tempest	William Shakespeare	Prospero	Harcourt Williams	
Oct	The Jealous Wife	George Colman	Lord Trinket	Harcourt Williams	
Nov	Antony and Cleopatra	William Shakespeare	Antony	Harcourt Williams	

1931 The Old Vic Company at the Old Vic Theatre and Sadler's Wells Theatre

DATE	TITLE	PLAYWRIGHT	ROLE	DIRECTOR	THEATRE
Jan	Twelfth Night	William Shakespeare	Malvolio	Harcourt Williams	
Mar	Arms and the Man	Bernard Shaw	Major Sergius Seranoff	Harcourt Williams	
Mar	Much Ado About Nothing	William Shakespeare	Benedict	Harcourt Williams	
Apr	King Lear	William Shakespeare	Lear	Harcourt Williams	
May	The Good Companions	J.B. Priestley and Edward Knoblock, from J.B. Priestley's novel	Inigo Jollifant	Julian Wylie	His Majesty's
Nov	Musical Chairs	Ronald Mackenzie	Joseph Schindler	Theodore Komisarjevsky	Arts
1932 Apr	Musical Chairs	Ronald Mackenzie	Joseph Schindler	Theodore Komisarjevsky	Criterion
Jun	Richard of Bordeaux	Gordon Daviot	Richard	John Gielgud and Harcourt Williams	Arts
1933 Feb	Richard of Bordeaux	Gordon Daviot	Richard	John Gielgud	New
1934 Jul	The Maitlands	Ronald Mackenzie	Roger Maitland	Theodore Komisarjevsky	Wyndham's
Nov	Hamlet	William Shakespeare	Hamlet	John Gielgud	New
1935 Jul	Noah	André Obey, translated by Arthur Wilmurt	Noah	Michel Saint-Denis	New
Oct	Romeo and Juliet	William Shakespeare	Mercutio	John Gielgud	New
Nov	Romeo and Juliet	William Shakespeare	Romeo	John Gielgud	New
1936 May	The Seagull	Anton Chekhov, translated by Theodore Komisarjevsky	Boris Trigorin	Theodore Komisarjevsky	New
Sep	Hamlet	William Shakespeare	Hamlet	Guthrie McClintic	Royal Alexandra, Toronto
Oct	Hamlet	William Shakespeare	Hamlet	Guthrie McClintic	Empire, New York
1937 Jan	Hamlet	William Shakespeare	Hamlet	Guthrie McClintic	St James's, New York
Feb	Hamlet	William Shakespeare	Hamlet	Guthrie McClintic	Shubert, Boston
May	He Was Born Gay	Emlyn Williams	Mason	John Gielgud and Emlyn Williams	Queen's
May	Nijinsky Matinée	poem by Christopher Hassall			His Majesty's

DATE	TITLE	PLAYWRIGHT	ROLE	DIRECTOR	THEATRE
1937/1938 John Gielgud Season at the Queen's Theatre					
Sep	Richard II	William Shakespeare	Richard	John Gielgud	
Nov	The School for Scandal	Richard Brinsley Sheridan	Joseph Surface	Tyrone Guthrie	
1938 Jan	Three Sisters	Anton Chekhov, translated by Constance Garnett	Vershinin	Michel Saint-Denis	
Apr	The Merchant of Venice	William Shakespeare	Shylock	John Gielgud and Glen Byam Shaw	
Sep	Dear Octopus	Dodie Smith	Nicholas	Glen Byam Shaw	Queen's
1939 Jan	The Importance of Being Earnest	Oscar Wilde	John Worthing	John Gielgud	Globe
Jun	Hamlet	William Shakespeare	Hamlet	John Gielgud	Lyceum
Jul	Hamlet	William Shakespeare	Hamlet	John Gielgud	Kronborg Castle, Elsinore
Aug	The Importance of Being Earnest	Oscar Wilde	John Worthing	John Gielgud	Globe
Oct	Shakespeare in Peace and War	William Shakespeare	lecture-recital		Bristol and Oxford
1940 Jan	Shakespeare in Peace and War	William Shakespeare	lecture-recital		Brighton and London
Mar	The Beggar's Opera	John Gay	Macheath (standing in for Michael Redgrave)	John Gielgud	Theatre Royal, Haymarket
Apr	King Lear	William Shakespeare	Lear	Lewis Casson and Harley Granville-Barker	Old Vic
May	The Tempest	William Shakespeare	Prospero	George Devine and Marius Goring	Old Vic
Jul	Fumed Oak	Noel Coward	Henry Crow	John Gielgud	Globe
	Hands Across the Sea	Noel Coward	Cmdr Peter Gilpin	John Gielgud	Globe
	Hard Luck Story	Anton Chekhov, adapted from Swan Song by John Gielgud	An old actor	John Gielgud	Globe
The three one-act plays went on a tour of camps for ENSA					
Aug	The Dark Lady of the Sonnets	Bernard Shaw	William Shakespeare	John Gielgud	Edinburgh (ENSA)
1941 Jan	Dear Brutus	J.M. Barrie	William Dearth	John Gielgud	Globe
1942 Jan	Macbeth	William Shakespeare	Macbeth	John Gielgud	tour
Jul	Macbeth	William Shakespeare	Macbeth	John Gielgud	Piccadilly
Oct	The Importance of Being Earnest	Oscar Wilde	John Worthing	John Gielgud	Globe
Dec/Jan	ENSA tour revue	various	various		Gibraltar
1943 Jan	The Doctor's Dilemma	Bernard Shaw	Louis Dubedat (standing in for Peter Glenville)	Irene Hentschel	Theatre Royal, Haymarket
Apr	Love for Love	William Congreve	Valentine	John Gielgud	Phoenix
1944/1945 John Gielgud Season at the Theatre Royal, Haymarket					
Oct	The Circle	Somerset Maugham	Arnold Champion-Chesney	William Armstrong	
Oct	Love for Love	William Congreve	Valentine	John Gielgud	
Oct	Hamlet	William Shakespeare	Hamlet	George Rylands	
1945 Jan	A Midsummer Night's Dream	William Shakespeare	Oberon	Nevill Coghill	
Apr	The Duchess of Malfi	John Webster	Ferdinand	George Rylands	
1945/1946 ENSA Tour of the Far East					
Oct/Feb	Hamlet	William Shakespeare	Hamlet	John Gielgud	
Oct/Feb	Blithe Spirit	Noel Coward	Charles Condomine	John Gielgud	
The tour included: Bombay, Deolali, Madras, Trincomalee, Colombo, Singapore, Saigon, Hong Kong, Rangoon, Delhi, Cawnpore, Karachi and Cairo					
	Shakespeare in Time of War and Peace	Lecture-recital			Colombo only
1946 Jun	Crime and Punishment	Fydor Dostoyevsky, dramatised by Rodney Ackland	Raskolnikoff	Anthony Quayle	New
Sep	Crime and Punishment	Fydor Dostoyevsky, dramatised by Rodney Ackland	Raskolnikoff	Anthony Quayle	Globe
1947 Tour of Canada and the United States					
Jan/Feb	The Importance of Being Earnest	Oscar Wilde	John Worthing	John Gielgud	
The production was seen in London (Ontario), Montreal, Toronto, Boston and Baltimore					

DATE	TITLE	PLAYWRIGHT	ROLE	DIRECTOR	THEATRE
Mar	The Importance of Being Earnest	Oscar Wilde	John Worthing	John Gielgud	Royale, New York
May	Love for Love	William Congreve	Valentine	John Gielgud	National, Washington
	Love for Love	William Congreve	Valentine	John Gielgud	Boston
Oct	Medea	Euripides, adapted by Robinson Jeffers	Jason	John Gielgud	National, New York
Dec	Crime and Punishment	Fydor Dostoyevsky, dramatised by Rodney Ackland	Raskolnikoff	Theodore Komisarjevsky	National, New York
1948 Nov	The Return of the Prodigal	St John Hankin	Eustace Jackson	Peter Glenville	Globe
1949 May	The Lady's Not For Burning	Christopher Fry	Thomas Mendip	John Gielgud and Esme Percy	Globe

1950 Shakespeare Memorial Theatre, Statford-upon-Avon

DATE	TITLE	PLAYWRIGHT	ROLE	DIRECTOR	THEATRE
Mar	Measure for Measure	William Shakespeare	Angelo	Peter Brook	
May	Julius Caesar	William Shakespeare	Cassius	Anthony Quayle and Michael Langham	
Jun	Much Ado About Nothing	William Shakespeare	Benedict	John Gielgud	
Jul	King Lear	William Shakespeare	Lear	John Gielgud and Anthony Quayle with acknowledgements to the late Harley Granville-Barker	
1951 Jan	The Lady's Not For Burning	Christopher Fry	Thomas Mendip	John Gielgud and Esme Percy	Royale, New York
Aug	The Winter's Tale	William Shakespeare	Leontes	Peter Brook	Phoenix
1952 Jan	Much Ado About Nothing	William Shakespeare	Benedict	John Gielgud	Phoenix

1953 John Gielgud Season at the Lyric Theatre, Hammersmith

DATE	TITLE	PLAYWRIGHT	ROLE	DIRECTOR	THEATRE
Feb	The Way of the World	William Congreve	Mirabell	John Gielgud	
May	Venice Preserv'd	Thomas Otway	Jaffeir	Peter Brook	
Jun	Stars at Midnight	lyric by Noel Coward			Palladium
Jul	Richard II	William Shakespeare	Richard	John Gielgud	Bulawayo
Nov	A Day by the Sea	N.C. Hunter	Julian Anson	John Gielgud	Theatre Royal, Haymarket

1955 Shakespeare Memorial Theatre in Europe and London

DATE	TITLE	PLAYWRIGHT	ROLE	DIRECTOR	THEATRE
Jun	King Lear	William Shakespeare	Lear	John Gielgud and George Devine	Europe and Palace
Jul	Much Ado About Nothing	William Shakespeare	Benedict	John Gielgud	Palace only

The tour included Vienna, Zurich, The Hague, Amsterdam, Rotterdam, Berlin, Copenhagen, Hanover, Oslo, Bremen and Hamburg.

DATE	TITLE	PLAYWRIGHT	ROLE	DIRECTOR	THEATRE
1956 Nov	Nude with Violin	Noel Coward	Sebastien	John Gielgud and Noel Coward	Globe
1957 Aug	The Tempest	William Shakespeare	Prospero	Peter Brook	Memorial, Stratford-upon-Avon
Sep	Ages of Man	William Shakespeare, based on anthology by George Rylands	solo recital		Edinburgh
Dec	The Tempest	William Shakespeare	Prospero	Peter Brook	Theatre Royal, Drury Lane
1958 Feb	The Potting Shed	Graham Greene	James Callifer	Michael MacOwan	Globe
May	Henry VIII	William Shakespeare	Cardinal Wolsey	Michael Benthall	Old Vic

The production was also seen in Paris, Antwerp and Brussels

DATE	TITLE	PLAYWRIGHT	ROLE	DIRECTOR	THEATRE
Jun	Ages of Man	William Shakespeare, based on anthology by George Rylands	solo recital		Bath
Sep/Dec	Ages of Man	William Shakespeare, based on anthology by George Rylands	solo recital		tour

The tour included 60 cities in Can ida and USA

DATE	TITLE	PLAYWRIGHT	ROLE	DIRECTOR	THEATRE
Dec	Ages of Man	William Shakespeare, based on anthology by George Rylands	solo recital		Spoleto and Venice
1959 Jun/Jul	Ages of Man	William Shakespeare, based on anthology by George Rylands	solo recital		Queen's
Sep	Much Ado About Nothing	William Shakespeare	Benedict	John Gielgud	Cambridge Drama Festival, Boston
Sep	Much Ado About Nothing	William Shakespeare	Benedict	John Gielgud	Lunt-Fontanne, New York

DATE	TITLE	PLAYWRIGHT	ROLE	DIRECTOR	THEATRE
1960					
Apr	Ages of Man	William Shakespeare, based on anthology by George Rylands	solo recital		Theatre Royal, Haymarket
Sep	The Last Joke	Enid Bagnold	Prince Ferdinand Cavanati	Glen Byam Shaw	Phoenix
1961					
Sep	Ages of Man	William Shakespeare, based on anthology by George Rylands	solo recital		Royal Shakespeare
Oct	Othello	William Shakespeare	Othello	Franco Zeffirelli	Royal Shakespeare
Dec	The Cherry Orchard	Anton Chekhov, in a version by John Gielgud	Gaev	Michel Saint-Denis	Aldwych
1962					
Apr	Ages of Man	William Shakespeare, based on anthology by George Rylands	solo recital		tour
The tour included Edinburgh, Liverpool, Cambridge and Brighton					
Jul	Ages of Man	William Shakespeare, based on anthology by George Rylands	solo recital		Malvern
Aug	Ages of Man	William Shakespeare, based on anthology by George Rylands			tour
The tour included Tel Aviv, Jerusalem, Haifa, Ein Hashofet and Dublin					
Oct	The School for Scandal	Richard Brinsley Sheridan	Joseph Surface	John Gielgud	Theatre Royal, Haymarket
Dec	The School for Scandal	Richard Brinsley Sheridan	Joseph Surface	John Gielgud	Majestic, New York
The production also visited Toronto, Philadelphia and Washington					
1963					
Jan	Ages of Man	William Shakespeare, based on anthology by George Rylands	solo recital		Majestic, New York
Apr	Ages of Man	William Shakespeare, based on anthology by George Rylands	solo recital		Lyceum, New York
Aug	The Ides of March	Thornton Wilder, adapted by Jerome Kilty	Julius Caesar	John Gielgud and Jerome Kilty	Theatre Royal, Haymarket
Nov/Jan	Ages of Man	William Shakespeare, based on anthology by George Rylands	solo recital		tour
The tour included Perth, Adelaide, Brisbane, Melbourne, Wellington, Auckland and Christchurch					
1964					
Feb	Hamlet	William Shakespeare	Ghost (recorded voice)	John Gielgud	O'Keefe Centre, Toronto
Mar	Homage to Shakespeare	William Shakespeare	recital		Lincoln Centre, New York
Mar	Homage to Shakespeare	William Shakespeare	recital		McCarter, Princeton University
Mar	Hamlet	William Shakespeare	Ghost (recorded voice)	John Gielgud	Shubert, New York
Mar	Homage to Shakespeare	William Shakespeare	recital		Philharmonic Hall, New York
Apr	Ages of Man	William Shakespeare, based on anthology by George Rylands	solo recital		Playhouse, Nottingham
May	Ages of Man	William Shakespeare, based on anthology by George Rylands	solo recital		tour
The tour included Stockholm, Copenhagen, Warsaw, Helsinki, Leningrad and Moscow					
Sep	Ages of Man	William Shakespeare, based on anthology by George Rylands	solo recital		Dublin
Dec	Tiny Alice	Edward Albee	Julian	Alan Schneider	Billy Rose, New York
1965					
Mar	Ages of Man	William Shakespeare, based on anthology by George Rylands	solo recital		The Whitehouse, Washington
Sep	Ivanov	Anton Chekhov, adapted by John Gielgud from translation by Adriadne Nickolaeff	Ivanov	John Gielgud	Phoenix
1966					
May	Ivanov	Anton Chekhov, adapted by John Gielgud from translation by Adriadne Nickolaeff	Ivanov	John Gielgud	Shubert, New York
Oct	Ages of Man	William Shakespeare, based on anthology by George Rylands	solo recital		Norway
Nov/Jan	Men, Women and Shakespeare	William Shakespeare	recital		tour
The tour included São Paulo, Rio de Janeiro, Montevideo, Buenos Aires, Santiago de Chile, Washington, Chicago, Boston, Indianapolis, New York and South Orange.					
1967					
Jan	Ages of Man	William Shakespeare, based on anthology by George Rylands	solo recital		Los Angeles
Mar	Oedipus Rex	Igor Stravinsky	Narrator	Georg Solti	Festival Hall
Jun	Ages of Man	William Shakespeare, based on anthology by George Rylands	solo recital		Ankara
Nov	Tartuffe	Molière, translated by Richard Wilbur	Orgon	Tyrone Guthrie	Old Vic (NT)

DATE	TITLE	PLAYWRIGHT	ROLE	DIRECTOR	THEATRE
1968 Mar	Oedipus	Seneca, adapted by Ted Hughes from translation by A.D. Turner	Oedipus	Peter Brook	Old Vic (NT)
Oct	40 Years On	Alan Bennett	Headmaster	Patrick Garland	Apollo
1970 Feb	The Battle of Shrivings	Peter Shaffer	Sir Gideon Petrie	Peter Hall	Lyric
Jun	Home	David Storey	Harry	Lindsay Anderson	Royal Court
Jul	Home	David Storey	Harry	Lindsay Anderson	Apollo
Nov	Home	David Storey	Harry	Lindsay Anderson	Morosco, New York
1971 Jul	Caesar and Cleopatra	Bernard Shaw	Caesar	Robin Phillips	Chichester
1972 Mar	O.W. (ballet)	Oscar Wilde	Voice only	Joe Layton	Sadler's Wells
Mar	Veterans	Charles Wood	Sir Geoffrey Kendle	Ronald Eyre	Royal Court
1974 Mar	The Tempest	William Shakespeare	Prospero	Peter Hall	Old Vic (NT)
Aug	Bingo	Edward Bond	William Shakespeare	Jane Howell and John Dove	Royal Court
1975 Apr	No Man's Land	Harold Pinter	Spooner	Peter Hall	Old Vic (NT)
Jul	No Man's Land	Harold Pinter	Spooner	Peter Hall	Wyndham's
1976 Feb	Tribute to the Lady	devised by Val May		Val May	Old Vic
Apr	No Man's Land	Harold Pinter	Spooner	Peter Hall	National
Nov	No Man's Land	Harold Pinter	Spooner	Peter Hall	Longacre, New York

1977/78 National Theatre

DATE	TITLE	PLAYWRIGHT	ROLE	DIRECTOR	THEATRE
1977 Jan	No Man's Land	Harold Pinter	Spooner	Peter Hall	Lyttelton
Mar	Julius Caesar	William Shakespeare	Caesar	John Schlesinger	Olivier
Apr	Volpone	Ben Jonson	Sir Politic Wouldbe	Peter Hall	Olivier
Nov	Half-Life	Julian Mitchell	Sir Noel Cunliffe	Waris Hussein	Cottesloe
1978 Mar	Half-Life	Julian Mitchell	Sir Noel Cunliffe	Waris Hussein	Duke of York's
1988 Jan	The Best of Friends	Hugh Whitemore	Sir Sydney Cockerell	James Roose-Evans	Apollo

FILM

DATE	FILM	ROLE	SCREENPLAY	DIRECTOR
1924	Who is the Man?	Daniel Arnault	adapted from *Daniel* by Louis Verneuil	Walter Summers
1926	Michael Strogoff	Michael Strogoff	Jules Verne	Theodore Komisarjevsky
1929	The Clue of the New Pin	Rex Trasmere	Edgar Wallace	Arthur Maude
1933	Insult	Henri Dubois	Jan Fabricus	Harry Lachman
	The Good Companions	Inigo Jollifant	W.P. Lipscombe, Anguls Macphail and Ian Dalrymple, based on novel by J.B. Priestley	Victor Saville
1934	Full Fathom Five	Voice only		Len Lye
1936	The Secret Agent	Ashenden	Charles Bennett, from play by Campbell Dixon adapted from Somerset Maugham's *The Traitor* and *The Hairless Mexican*	Alfred Hitchcock
1941	The Prime Minister	Benjamin Disraeli	Brock Williams and Michael Hogan	Thorold Dickenson
	An Airman's Letter to his Mother	Voice only		Michael Powell
1943	Unfinished journey	Narrator		Eugene Cekalski
1944	Shakespeare's Country	Narrator		Lister Lawrence
1945	A Diary for Timothy	Hamlet	William Shakespeare	Humphrey Jennings
1953	Julius Caesar	Cassius	William Shakespeare	Joseph L. Mankiewicz
1954	Romeo and Juliet	Prologue	adapted by Renato Castellani	Renato Castellani
1955	Richard III	Clarence	William Shakespeare, adapted by Laurence Olivier and Alan Dent	Laurence Olivier
1957	The Barretts of Wimpole Street	Edward Moulton-Barrett	John Dighton, from play by Rudolf Besier	Sidney Franklin
	Saint Joan	Earl of Warwick	Graham Greene, from play by Bernard Shaw	Otto Preminger
	Around the World in Eighty Days	Foster	James Poe, S.J. Perelman and John Farrow, based on novel by Jules Verne	Michael Anderson

FILM

DATE	FILM	ROLE	SCREENPLAY	DIRECTOR
1958	The Immortal Land	Voice only	George Seferis	Basil Wright
1964	Becket	Louis VII	Edward Anhalt, based on play by Jean Anouilh	Peter Glenville
1965	The Loved One	Sir Francis Hinsley	Terry Southern and Christopher Isherwood, based on novel by Evelyn Waugh	Tony Richardson
1966	Campanadas a Medianoche (English title: Chimes at Midnight)	Henry IV	Orson Welles, based on passages from *Richard II, Henry IV Parts I and II* and *The Merry Wives of Windsor* by William Shakespeare	Orson Welles
1967	Assignment to Kill	Curt Valayan	Sheldon Reynolds	Sheldon Reynolds
	To Die in Madrid	Narrator	Madeleine Chapsal. English version: Helen Scott	English version: George Gonnea
	October Revolution	Narrator	Madeleine Chapsal. English version: Constantine Fitzgibbon	English version: Constantine Fitzgibbon
1968	Sebastian	Head of Intelligence	Gerald Vaughan-Hughes, based on original screenplay by Leo Marks	David Greene
	The Charge of the Light Brigade	Lord Raglan	Charles Wood	Tony Richardson
	The Shoes of the Fisherman	The Pope	John Patrick, based on Morris L. West's novel	Michael Anderson
1969	Oh! What a Lovely War	Count Berchtold	Len Deighton, from Joan Littlewood's stage production, based on *The Long Trail* by Charles Chilton	Richard Attenborough
1970	Julius Caesar	Caesar	William Shakespeare	Stuart Burge
	Eagle in a Cage	Lord Sissal	Millard Lampell	Fielder Cook
1973	The Lost Horizon	Chang	Larry Kramer, from novel by James Hilton	Charles Jarrott
1974	11 Harrowhouse	Meecham	Jeffrey Bloom, adapted by Charles Grodin, based on novel by Gerald A. Browne	Aram Avakian
	Gold	Farrell	Wilbur Smith and Stanley Price, based on novel *Goldmine* by Wilbur Smith	Peter Hunt
	Frankenstein: The True Story	Chief Constable	Christopher Isherwood and Don Bachardy, from novel by Mary W. Shelley	Jack Smight
	Murder on the Orient Express	Beddoes	Paul Dehn, from novel by Agatha Christie	Sidney Lumet
	Galileo	Old Cardinal	Barbara Bray and Joseph Losey, from the English version of Bertolt Brecht's play by Charles Laughton	Joseph Losey
1976	Aces High	Headmaster	Howard Barker, inspired by R.C. Sherriff's play *Journey's End*	Jack Gold
1977	Providence	Clive Langham	David Mercer	Alain Resnais
	Joseph Andrews	Doctor	Allan Scott and Chris Bryant. Screenstory by Tony Richardson based on novel by Henry Fielding	Tony Richardson
1979	Caligula	Nerva	Gore Vidal	Tinto Brass, Giancarlo Lui, Bob Guccione, Franco Rossellini
	Portrait of the Artist as a Young Man	Preacher	Judith Rascoe, from novel by James Joyce	Joseph Strick
	Murder by Decree	Lord Salisbury	John Hopkins, based on *The Ripper File* by John Lloyd and Elwyn Jones	Bob Clark
1980	The Human Factor	Brigadier Tomlinson	Tom Stoppard, from novel by Graham Greene	Otto Preminger
	The Elephant Man	Carr Gomm	Eric Begren, Christopher de Vore and David Lynch	David Lynch
1981	Dyrygent (English title: The Conductor)	Jan Lasocki	Andrzej Kijowski, based on notes by Andrzej Markowski	Andrzej Wajda
	Omar Mukhtar – Lion of the Desert	Sharif El Gariani	H.A.L. Craig	Moustapha Akkad
	Sphinx	Abdu Hamdi	John Byrum, from novel by Robin Cook	Franklin J. Shaffner
	Chariots of Fire	Master of Trinity	Colin Welland	Hugh Hudson
	The Formula	Dr Abraham Esau	Steve Shagan	John G. Avildsen
	Arthur	Hobson	Steve Gordon	Steve Gordon
	Priest of Love	Herbert G. Muskett	Alan Plater, based on Harry T. Moore's biography	Christopher Miles
1982	Buddenbrooks	Narrator	Bernt Rothert, Hans Joachim Lange and Franz Peter Wirth, based on novel by Thomas Mann	Franz Peter Wirth English version: George Spenton Foster
	Gandhi	Lord Irwin	John Briley	Richard Attenborough
	Invitation to the Wedding	Clyde Ormiston	William Fairchild, from story treatment by Joseph Brooks, William Fairchild and Miss Paul	Joseph Brooks
	The Wicked Lady	Hogarth	Leslie Arliss and Michael Winner, additional dialogue by Gordon Glennon and Aimee Stuart, from the book *Life and Death of The Wicked Lady Skelton* by Magdalen King-Hall	Michael Winner
	Scandalous	Uncle Willie	Rob Cohen and John Byrum	Rob Cohen
1985	The Shooting Party	Cornelius Cardew	Julian Bond, from novel by Isabel Colegate	Alan Bridges
	Wagner	Pfistermeister	Charles Wood	Tony Palmer
	Plenty	Sir Leonard Darwin	David Hare	Fred Schepisi

DATE	FILM	ROLE	SCREENPLAY	DIRECTOR
1986	Leave All Fair	John Middleton Murry	Stanley Harper, Maurice Pons, Jean Betts and John Reid	John Reid
1987	The Whistle Blower	Sir Adrian Chapple	Julian Bond, from novel by John Hale	Simon Langton
1988	Bluebeard, Bluebeard	Bluebeard	Fabio Carpi	Fabio Carpi
	Appointment with Death	Colonel Carbury	Michael Winner, Peter Buckman and Anthony Shaffer, based on novel by Agatha Christie	Michael Winner
	Arthur on the Rocks	Hobson	Andy Breckman	Bud Yorkin

TELEVISION

DATE	TITLE	ROLE	WRITER	DIRECTOR	COMPANY
1959	The Browning Version	Andrew Crocker-Harris	Terence Rattigan	John Frankenheimer	CBS
	A Day by the Sea	Julian Anson	N.C. Hunter	Lionel Harris	ATV
1962	The Cherry Orchard	Gaev	Anton Chekhov, version by John Gielgud	Michael Elliott from Michel Saint-Denis's RSC production	BBC
1963	The Rehearsal	The Count	Jean Anouilh, translated by Pamela Hansford Johnson and Kitty Black, adapted for TV by G.C. Brown	Graham Evans	ATV
	Farewell to the Vic	interview		David Jones	BBC
1964	Hamlet	Ghost	William Shakespeare	John Gielgud	Electronicvision
1966	Great Acting	interview		Hal Burton	BBC
	Ivanov	Ivanov	Anton Chekhov, adapted for television by John Bowen from stage adaptation by John Gielgud, based on original translation by Ariadne Nicolaeff	Graham Evans	ATV
	Conflict	Presenter	Ivor Brown	George More O'Ferral	BBC
	The Love Song of Barney Kempinski	Stockbroker	Murray Shisgal	Stanley Prager	ABC (USA)
	The Ages of Man	Recital	William Shakespeare	Paul Bogart	CBS
	The Mayfly and the Frog	Gabriel Kantara	Jack Russell	Robin Midgley	BBC
	Alice in Wonderland	Mock Turtle	Lewis Carroll	Jonathan Miller	BBC
1967	Romeo and Juliet	Prologue	William Shakespeare	Alan Cooke	BBC
1968	From Chekhov with Love	Chekhov	translated by Moura Budberg and Gordon Latta, adapted and staged by Jonathan Miller	Bill Turner	Rediffusion
	Saint Joan	Inquisitor	Bernard Shaw	Basil Coleman	BBC
1969	Conversation at Night	The Writer	Friedrich Durrenmatt, translated by Robert David MacDonald	Rudolph Cartier	BBC
	The Actor's Changing Face	interview		Hal Burton	BBC
1970	In Good King Charles's Golden Days	Charles II	Bernard Shaw	Basil Coleman	BBC
	Carol Channing's Mad English Tea Party	Guest Star	Ron Friedman and Bryan Blackburn, Ilson and Chambers	Colin Clews	ITC
1971	Hassan	Caliph	James Elroy Flecker, adapted for television by Rex Tucker from stage version by Basil Dean	Rex Tucker	BBC
	Hamlet	Ghost	William Shakespeare	Peter Wood	ATV
	Fifty Years On	interview		Hal Burton	BBC
1972	Probe	Streeter		Russell Mayberry	Warner Bros TV
	Home	Harry	David Storey	Lindsay Anderson	CBS/BBC
1973	This Is Noel Coward	Narrator	Charles Castle	Charles Castle	ITV
	William	Narrator	Hildy Parks	Ian MacNaughton	ABC
	Deliver Us From Evil	Frederick William Densham	Hugh Whitemore	David Sullivan Proudfoot	BBC
	Life of Leonardo da Vinci	Narrator	Renato Castellani	Renato Castellani	NBC
	QB VII	Clinton-Meek	Edward Anhalt, based on novel by Leon Uris	Tom Gries	Columbia TV
1975	Special Duties	Mr Ferraro	Graham Greene, adapted by John Mortimer	Alastair Reid	Thames

DATE	TITLE	ROLE	WRITER	DIRECTOR	COMPANY
	Edward VII	Benjamin Disraeli	David Butler, based on Sir Philip Mangnus's biography	John Gorrie	ATV
1976	Voyage to the End of the Earth	Narrator	John Palmer	Michael Bortman	WETA-PBS
	Peter Pan	Narrator	Andrew Birkin and Jack Burns, based on J.M. Barrie's play	Dwight Hemion	ITC-NBC
	Your National Theatre	interview		Derek Bailey	LWT
	The Picture of Dorian Gray	Lord Henry Wotton	Oscar Wilde, dramatised by John Osborne	John Gorrie	BBC
1977	The Grand Inquisitor	The Grand Inquisitor	Fedor Dostoyevsky	Richard Argent	BBC Open University
	Heartbreak House	Captain Shotover	Bernard Shaw	Cedric Messina	BBC
	The Pallisers	Host for US transmission	Anthony Trollope, dramatised by Simon Raven	Hugh David	BBC
1978	Neck	Jelks	Roald Dahl, dramatised by Robin Chapman	Christopher Miles	Anglia
	No Man's Land	Spooner	Harold Pinter	Julian Amyes adapted from Peter Hall's NT production	Granada
	Richard II	John of Gaunt	William Shakespeare	David Giles	BBC
	Romeo and Juliet	Prologue	William Shakespeare	Alvin Rakoff	BBC
1980	Why Didn't They Ask Evans?	Rev. Thomas Jones	Agatha Christie, adapted by Pat Sandys	Tony Wharmby	LWT
	The English Garden	Presenter	Alan Gore and Laurence Fleming	Richard Mervyn	Thames
	Les Misérables	Gillenormand	John Gay, adapted from Victor Hugo's novel	Glenn Jordan	Thames
	Parson's Pleasure	Cyril Boggis	Roald Dahl, dramatised by Ronald Harwood	John Bruce	Anglia
1981	The Seven Dials Mystery	Marquis of Caterham	Agatha Christie, dramatised by Pat Sandys	Tony Wharmby	LWT
	Brideshead Revisited	Edward Ryder	Evelyn Waugh, dramatised by John Mortimer	Charles Sturridge and Michael Lindsay-Hogg	Granada
1982	The Hunchback of Notre Dame	Torturer	John Gay, adapted from Victor Hugo's novel	Michael Tuchner	CBS
	The Critic	Lord Burleigh	Richard Brinsley Sheridan	Don Taylor	BBC
1983	The Scarlet and the Black	Pope Pius XII	David Butler, based on J.P. Gallagher's *The Scarlet Pimpernel of the Vatican*	Jerry London	ITC
	Inside the Third Reich	Albert Speer Sr	E. Jack Neuman	Martin Chomsky	ABC
1984	The Far Pavilions	Major Sir Louis Cavagnari	Julian Bond, adapted from the novel by M.M.Kaye	Peter Duffell	Goldcrest
	All The World's A Stage	interview	Ronald Harwood	Harry Hastings and Mischa Williams	BBC
	The Master of Ballantrae	Lord Durrisdeer	Robert Louis Stevenson, adapted by William Bast	Douglas Hickox	HTV
	Six Centuries of Verse	Presenter		Richard Mervyn	Thames
	Frankenstein	De Lacey	Victor Gialanella, from the novel by Mary Shelley	James Ormerod	Yorkshire
	Camille	The Duke de Charles	Blanche Hanalis, based on Alexander Dumas's *The Lady of the Camelias*	Desmond Davis	CBS
1985	Romance on the Orient Express	Charles Woodward	Jan Worthington	Lawrence Gordon Clark	Yorkshire
1986	Time After Time	Jasper Swift	Andrew Davies, adapted from Molly Keane's novel	Bill Hays	BBC
	A Marriage of Convenience	interview		Richard Attenborough	Thames
	Marco Polo	Doge	David Butler, Vincenzo Labella and Giuliano Montaldo	Giuliano Montaldo	People's Republic of China
	Oedipus the King	Teiresias	Sophocles, translated by Don Taylor	Don Taylor	BBC
	Antigone	Teiresias	Sophocles, translated by Don Taylor	Don Taylor	BBC
1987	Quartermaine's Terms	Eddie Loomis	Simon Gray	Bill Hays	BBC
	The Canterville Ghost	Sir Simon de Canterville	Oscar Wilde, adapted by Sue Grafton, Steve Humphrey and George Zatesco	Paul Bogart	HTV
1988	War and Remembrance	Dr Aaron Jastrow	Herman Wouk	Dan Curtis	ABC

DIRECTOR

DATE	TITLE	PLAYWRIGHT	THEATRE
1932			
Feb	Romeo and Juliet	William Shakespeare	New, Oxford (OUDS)
June	Richard of Bordeaux*†	Gordon Daviot	Arts
Sep	Strange Orchestra	Rodney Ackland	St Martin's
Dec	The Merchant of Venice	William Shakespeare	Old Vic
1933			
Feb	Richard of Bordeaux*	Gordon Daviot	New
Sep	Sheppey	W. Somerset Maugham	Wyndham's
1934			
Jan	Spring 1600†	Emlyn Williams	Shaftesbury
Jun	Queen of Scots	Gordon Daviot	New
Nov	Hamlet*	William Shakespeare	New
1935			
Apr	The Old Ladies	Rodney Ackland, adapted from novel by Hugh Walpole	New
Oct	Romeo and Juliet*	William Shakespeare	New
Nov	Romeo and Juliet*	William Shakespeare	New
Nov	Punch cartoons	George du Maurier	His Majesty's
1936			
Feb	Richard II	William Shakespeare	New, Oxford (OUDS)
1937			
May	He Was Born Gay*†	Emlyn Williams	Queen's
Sep	Richard II*	William Shakespeare	Queen's
1938			
Apr	The Merchant of Venice*†	William Shakespeare	Queen's
May	Spring Meeting	M.J. Farrell and John Perry	Ambassadors
1939			
Jan	The Importance of Being Earnest*	Oscar Wilde	Globe
Apr	Scandal in Assyria	Axel Kjellstrom, adapted Gerald Bullett	Globe
May	Rhondda Roundabout	Jack Jones	Globe
Jun	Hamlet*	William Shakespeare	Lyceum
Jul	Hamlet*	William Shakespeare	Kronborg Castle, Elsinore
Aug	The Importance of Being Earnest*	Oscar Wilde	Globe
1940			
Mar	The Beggar's Opera*	John Gay	Theatre Royal, Haymarket
Jul	Fumed Oak*	Noel Coward	Globe and ENSA tour
Jul	Hands Across the Sea*	Noel Coward	Globe and ENSA tour
Jul	Hard Luck Story*	Anton Chekhov, adapted from *Swan Song* by John Gielgud	Globe and ENSA tour
Aug	The Dark Lady of the Sonnets*	Bernard Shaw	Edinburgh
1941			
Jan	Dear Brutus*	J.M. Barrie	Globe
Nov	Ducks and Drakes	M.J. Farrell	Apollo
1942			
Jul	Macbeth*	William Shakespeare	Piccadilly
Oct	The Importance of Being Earnest*	Oscar Wilde	Phoenix
1943			
Apr	Love for Love*	William Congreve	Phoenix
Oct	Landslide	Dorothy Albertyn and David Peel	Westminster
1944			
Jan	The Cradle Song	Gregorio Martinez Sierra, translated by Helen and Harley Granville-Barker	Apollo
May	Crisis in Heaven	Eric Linklater	Lyric
Jun	The Last of Summer	Kate O'Brien and John Perry, from Kate O'Brien's novel	Phoenix
Oct	Love for Love*	William Congreve	Theatre Royal, Haymarket
1945			
Aug	Lady Windermere's Fan	Oscar Wilde	Theatre Royal, Haymarket
Oct	Hamlet*	William Shakespeare	ENSA tour
Oct	Blithe Spirit*	Noel Coward	ENSA tour
1947			
Mar	The Importance of Being Earnest*	Oscar Wilde	Royale, New York
May	Love for Love*	William Congreve	US tour
Oct	Medea*	Euripides, freely adapted by Robinson Jeffers	National, New York
1948			
Jul	The Glass Menagerie	Tennessee Williams	Theatre Royal, Haymarket

DATE	TITLE	PLAYWRIGHT	THEATRE
Aug	Medea	Euripides, freely adapted by Robinson Jeffers	Royal Lyceum, Edinburgh
Sep	Medea	Euripides, freely adapted by Robinson Jeffers	Globe
1949			
Feb	The Heiress	Ruth and Augustus Goetz, based on Henry James's *Washington Square*	Theatre Royal, Haymarket
Apr	Much Ado About Nothing	William Shakespeare	Memorial, Stratford-upon-Avon
May	The Lady's Not for Burning*†	Christopher Fry	Globe
Sep	Treasure Hunt	M.J. Farrell and John Perry	Apollo
1950			
Jan	Shall We Join the Ladies?	J.M. Barrie	Lyric, Hammersmith
Jan	The Boy with a Cart	Christopher Fry	Lyric, Hammersmith
Jun	Much Ado About Nothing*	William Shakespeare	Memorial, Stratford-upon-Avon
Jul	King Lear*†	William Shakespeare	Memorial, Statford-upon-Avon
1951			
Jan	The Lady's Not For Burning*†	Christopher Fry	Royale, New York
Dec	Indian Summer	Peter Watling	Criterion
1952			
Jan	Much Ado About Nothing*	William Shakespeare	Phoenix
Jan	Macbeth	William Shakespeare	Memorial, Stratford-upon-Avon
Dec	Richard II	William Shakespeare	Lyric, Hammersmith
1953			
Feb	The Way of the World*	William Congreve	Lyric, Hammersmith
Jul	Richard II*	William Shakespeare	Bulawayo
Nov	A Day by the Sea*	N.C. Hunter	Theatre Royal, Haymarket
1954			
Feb	Charley's Aunt	Brandon Thomas	New
May	The Cherry Orchard	Anton Chekhov, adapted by John Gielgud	Lyric, Hammersmith
1955			
Apr	Twelfth Night	William Shakespeare	Memorial, Stratford-upon-Avon
Jun	King Lear*†	William Shakespeare	European Tour and Palace
Jul	Much Ado About Nothing*	William Shakespeare	Palace
1956			
Apr	The Chalk Garden	Enid Bagnold	Theatre Royal, Haymarket
Nov	Nude with Violin*†	Noel Coward	Globe
1957			
Jun	The Trojans	Hector Berlioz	Royal Opera House, Covent Garden
1958			
Apr	Variation on a Theme	Terence Rattigan	Globe
Jul	Five Finger Exercise	Peter Shaffer	Comedy
1959			
Jun	The Complaisant Lover	Graham Greene	Globe
Sep	Much Ado About Nothing*	William Shakespeare	US tour
Dec	Five Finger Exercise	Peter Shaffer	Music Box, New York
1961			
Feb	A Midsummer Night's Dream	Michael Tippett	Royal Opera House, Covent Garden
Mar	Big Fish, Little Fish	Hugh Wheeler	ANTA, New York
Jun	Dazzling Prospect	M.J. Farrell and John Perry	Globe
1962			
Apr	The School for Scandal	Richard Brinsley Sheridan	Theatre Royal, Haymarket
Oct	The School for Scandal*	Richard Brinsley Sheridan	Theatre Royal, Haymarket
Dec	The School for Scandal*	Richard Brinsley Sheridan	Majestic, New York
1963			
Aug	The Ides of March*†	Thornton Wilder	Theatre Royal, Haymarket
1964			
Apr	Hamlet*	William Shakespeare	Lunt-Fontanne, New York
1965			
Sep	Ivanov*	Anton Chekhov, adapted by John Gielgud from translation by Ariadne Nicolaeff	Phoenix
1966			
May	Ivanov*	Anton Chekhov, adapted by John Gielgud from translation by Ariadne Nicolaeff	Shubert, New York
1967			
Nov	Half Way Up The Tree	Peter Ustinov	Queen's
1968			
Aug	Don Giovanni	Amadeus Wolfgang Mozart	Coliseum

DATE	TITLE	PLAYWRIGHT	THEATRE
1971 Apr	All Over	Edward Albee	Martin Beck, New York
1972 Sep	Private Lives	Noel Coward	Queen's
	Irene‡	Hugh Wheeler and Joseph Stein, Harry Tierney and Joseph McCarthy	US tour
1973 Sep	The Constant Wife	W. Somerset Maugham	Albery
1974 Sep	Private Lives	Noel Coward	US tour
Dec	The Constant Wife	W. Somerset Maugham	US tour
1975 Jan	The Gay Lord Quex	Arthur Wing Pinero	Albery

* In all these productions John Gielgud appeared
† Richard of Bordeaux co-directed with Harcourt Williams
‡ Spring 1600 co-directed with Emlyn Williams
‡ He Was Born Gay co-directed with Emlyn Williams
‡ The Merchant of Venice co-directed with Glen Byam Shaw
‡ The Lady's Not For Burning co-directed with Esme Percy

† King Lear (1950) co-directed with Anthony Quayle with acknowledgements to the late Harley Granville-Barker
‡ King Lear (1955) co-directed with George Devine
‡ Nude with Violin co-directed with Noel Coward
‡ Ides of March co-directed with Jerome Kilty
‡ Irene: Gielgud was sacked on the pre-Broadway tour

RECORDINGS

major recordings include:
Jean Anouilh
  Becket (RCA-Victor)
Max Beerbohm
  Zuleika Dobson (Argo)
Alan Bennett
  40 Years On (Decca)
Bible
  Readings from the Psalms (Argo)
John Bunyan
  The Pilgrim's Progress (Argo)
Anton Chekhov
  Gielgud's Chekhov (Master-Vision-Cassette)
Winston Churchill
  The Story of Sir Winston (Caedmon)
William Congreve
  The Way of the World (Angel)
  The Way of the World (Columbia)
  The Way of the World (Gramophone)
Charles Dickens
  Bleak House (Argo)
  A Tale of Two Cities (Argo)
Conan Doyle
  Doctor Watson Meets Sherlock (Decca)
  Holmes: The Final Solution
T.S. Eliot
  Old Possum's Book of Practical Cats (Caedmon)
Christopher Fry

  The Lady's Not for Burning (Decca)
Ben Jonson
  Volpone (NT production) (NSA*)
Julian Mitchell
  Half-Life (NT production) (NSA*)
Molière
  Tartuffe (NT production) (NSA*)
Harold Pinter
  No Man's Land (Caedmon)
  No Man's Land (NT production) (NSA*)
'Saki' (H.H. Munro)
  Tobermory and other short stories (Argo)
William Shakespeare
  Hamlet (Brunswick)
  Hamlet (CBS)
  Hamlet (excerpts) (Decca)
  Hamlet (HMV)
  Hamlet (RCA-Victor)
  Henry V (Caedmon)
  Julius Caesar (MFP)
  Julius Caesar (NT production) (NSA*)
  Measure for Measure (Caedmon)
  Much Ado About Nothing (Argo)
  Othello (Argo)
  Othello (Oldbourne Press)
  Richard II (Caedmon)
  Richard III (Gramophone)
  Romeo and Juliet (excerpts) (Decca)

  Sonnets (Caedmon)
  Sonnets (Decca)
  The Winter's Tale (Caedmon)
  The Winter's Tale (RCA-Victor)
Bernard Shaw
  Arms and the Man (abridged) (Talking Tape Co)
Richard Brinsley Sheridan
  The School for Scandal (Caedmon)
  The School for Scandal (Command)
Edith Sitwell
  Poems (RCA-Victor)
David Storey
  Home (Royal Court production) (NSA*)
Igor Stravinsky
  L'Histoire du Soldat (Deutsche Grammophon)
Jonathan Swift
  Gulliver's Travels (Argo)
Evelyn Waugh
  Brideshead Revisited (abridged) (Argo)
Oscar Wilde
  The Happy Prince (Nimbus)
  The Importance of Being Earnest (Angel)
  The Importance of Being Earnest (Columbia)
  The Importance of Being Earnest (MFP)

Charles Wood
  Veterans (Royal Court production) (NSA*)
Anthologies
  Ages of Man (Columbia)
  Ages of Man (Philips)
  A Box at the Caedmon Theatre (Caedmon)
  Homage to Shakespeare (Argo)
  Men and Women of Shakespeare (RCA-Victor)
  More Favourite Poems (Argo)
  One Man in His Time (Philips)
  People Past and Present (Fontana)
  People Past and Present (Fourfront)
  Shakespeare (Columbia)
  Shakespeare at Stratford (Argo)
  Shakespeare Selection (Argo)
  Shakespeare Series (Linguaphone)
  Sir John Gielgud in his Greatest Roles (BBC Disc)
  The Voice of Poetry (Columbia)
  We Were Happy There! (MCA)
  The World of Peggy Ashcroft and John Gielgud (Decca)
  The World of Shakespeare (Argo)
  Your Favourite Poems (Argo)

**NSA: National Sound Archives tape-recording*

RADIO

1929	The Man with a Flower in his Mouth German National Programme
1930	Scenes from Hamlet Readings from Richard II
1931	The Tempest Will Shakespeare
1932	Othello Hamlet
1933	The Tempest
1937	He Was Born Gay The School for Scandal
1939	The Importance of Being Earnest Hamlet
1940	Hamlet The Laughing Woman The Important of Being Earnest

1941	Hi Gang Scrapbook Prince of Bohemia King Lear My Life in the Theatre Women at War The Return of Mr Oakroyd
1945	The Great Ship Pilgrim's Progress
1946	Granville-Barker
1948	The Family Reunion Hamlet The Tempest
1949	The Wreck of the Deutschland Colonial Journey Alhambra of the Air

	Hero and Leander Parts I and II Return to the Old Vic
1951	The Importance of Being Earnest Interview with Igor Cassini The Cross and the Arrow King Lear Helena
1952	Valedictory Richard of Bordeaux Portrait of a Great Lady
1953	The Tempest Visit to Bulawayo
1954	Ivanov The Adventures of Sherlock Holmes The missing scene from The Importance of Being Earnest

1955 Scheherazade

1956 Present Laughter
      The Rime of the Ancient Mariner

1957 The Browning Version
      Ode on the Morning of Christ's nativity

1958 The Living Shakespeare
      Lycidas

1959 Oedipus at Colonus

1960 The Way of the World
      Profile on Richard Burton
      Richard II
      The John Mills Story

1961 Arms and the Man

1962 A Pride of Terrys
      Desert Island Discs
      The Butterfly that Stamped
      Studies of Poetry: A.E.Housman

1964 Shakespeare's Quatercentenary
      Shakespeare's Sonnets

1965 The Theatre in theThirties

1966 Travellers' Tales
      Recollection of Robert Farquharson
      In Memoriam

Portrait of George Devine

1967 King Lear
      Five Children With It
      Leon Quartermain

1968 Edith Evans Miscellany Programme

1969 Interview with John Geilgud
      Ellen Terry: Portrait of an Actress
      Lord Hervey's Memoirs
      Somerset Maugham in the Theatre
      Sir Lewis Casson

1970 Be My Guest
      I Don't Mind What They Do As Long As They
      Don't Do It In The Steets and Frighten The
      Horses
      The Time of My Life: Val Gielgud

1971 Two Knights Not A Round Table

1972 Darling Nelly
      Distinguished Company

1973 40 Years On

1974 Christmas Epilogue

1975 O Wild West Wind
      Pilgrim's Progress
      Mr Luby's Fear of Heaven

The Grand Inquisitor
Interview with John Gielgud and Ralph
Richardson

1976 Henry V
      Disraeli's Reminiscences
      Tribute to the Lady
      Treading the Boards

1977 Vivat Rex

1978 Themes from Childhood
      The Monogamist
      Ode to the West Wind
      Sir John Gielgud Talking

1980 Val Gielgud
      A Victorian Playgoer

1981 The Irving Inheritance
      Desert Island Discs
      Glory
      Leave It to Psmith
      Noel Edmond's Show: The Railway Series
      The Winter's Tale

1983 Passing Time
      Six Centuries of Verse

1984 Tribute to Richard Burton

All productions for the BBC

AWARDS AND HONOURS

1956 Stage, New York, Award: 'Palm' for Hamlet

1959 *Early Stages* published

1942- President of the Actors' Benevolent Fund

1950 Hon. LLD St Andrews University

1953 Created Knight Bachelor in the Coronation and Birthday Honours
      Hon. D.Litt Oxford University
      British Film Academy: Award for Best British Actor for Cassius in *Julius Caesar*

1957 Chevalier de la Légion d'Honneur

1958- President Shakespearian Reading Society

1959 Tony Award: Special Contribution to Theatre for his extraordinary insight into the writings of Shakespeare

1961 Elected Foreign Honorary Member to American Academy of Arts and Sciences, Boston, Massachusetts
      Tony Award: Best Director for *Big Fish, Little Fish*

1963 *Stage Directions* published

1965 Hon. LLD Bradeis University

1968 Variety Club of Great Britain Award for the Headmaster in *40 Years On*

1970 Evening Standard Drama Award: Joint Best Actor for Harry in *Home*

1972 *Distinguished Company* published

1974 Society of Film and Television Arts Award for Beddoes in *Murder on the Orient Express*

1975 Plays and Players Award for Spooner in *No Man's Land*

1977 Companion of Honour
      Hon.D.Litt London University

1977- President of RADA

1979 Elected to the Theatre Hall of Fame for outstanding contribution to New York Theatre
      The National Academy of Recording Arts and Sciences 'Grammy' for *Ages of Man*
      An Actor and His Time published

1980 Open University D.Univ

1982 Academy of Motion Pictures Arts and Sciences 'Oscar' for Hobson in *Arthur*
      Golden Globes Award for Hobson in *Arthur*
      New York Film Critics Circle Award for Hobson in *Arthur*
      Los Angeles Film Critics Award for Hobson in *Arthur*

1983 Standard Award: Special award to mark his 60 years of acting and lifetime of service to British stage
      The National Academy of Recording Arts and Sciences 'Grammy' for *Old Possum's Book of Practical Cats*

1985 Laurence Olivier Award: special award for services to theatre

1986 The National Academy of Recording Arts and Sciences 'Grammy' for *Gulliver's Travels*
      Los Angeles Film Critics Award for Sir Leonard Darwin in *Plenty* and Cornelius Cardew in *The Shooting Party*

1987/8 John Gielgud Exhibition at The Theatre Museum

ACKNOWLEDGEMENTS

The author would like to begin by thanking the contributors, the photographers, his editor Ian Hyde, his designer Hugh Schermuly and Tim Pearce of Harrap.

The author and publisher would like to express their appreciation to the following for their assistance and/or permission to reproduce the photographs. Every effort has been made to trace the copyright owners and the author and publisher would like to apologise to anyone whose copyright has been infringed.

ABC TV, 167; Action Films, 150; Anglia Television Limited, 155, 160 (top); Antony, 64; The Associated Press Limited, 105 (right); copyright BBC (Enterprises), 110 (right), 118, 120 (left), 124 (right), 150, 154 (top right), 144, 145, 151 (top), 153, 154 (bottom), 175 (top), 176; BBC Hulton Picture Library, 21, 25, 29, 38, 53, 55, 62, 63, 66, 94; Cecil Beaton courtesy of Sotheby's London, 2, 44, 46, 61, 68, 69, 70, 71, 72, 77; Alexander Bender, 75; British Lion, 27; Cannon Distributors, 169; Columbia Pictures Corporation, 154 (top left); Columbia/EMI/Warner Bros. 156 (bottom), 160 (bottom), 174; Commonwealth United, 127 (right); Contemporary Films, 156 (top); Anthony Crickmay, 140; Zoë Dominic, 121, 126, 158; EMI, 136 (top), 143; EMI/Paramount Pictures, 159; Enterprises, 161 (right); Financial Times, 146, 147; Friedman-Abeles, 106; collection Sir John Gielgud, 17, 18, 19, 20 (top), 22, 23, 26, 34 (top left and right), 37, 45, 49, 74, 117, 122; Granada Television Limited, 152, 165; Guild Entertainment Limited, 168 (left); John Haynes, 6, 125, 129, 133, 148; Hemdale Films, 136 (bottom); HTV Limited, 172 (top), 177 (top); ITC Entertainment Limited, 105 (left), 152, 142, 151 (bottom), 168 (right); Ely Landau, 135; London Trust Cultural Productions Limited, 170 (bottom); London Weekend Television Limited, 158 (top right), 161 (left); Raymond Mander and Joe Mitchenson Theatre Collection, 24, 28, 30, 32, 34 (bottom), 35, 36, 47; Angus McBean, courtesy Harvard Theater Collection, 56, 59, 60, 78, 80, 81, 82, 83, 84, 85, 86, 87, 88, 90, 92, 99, 100, 103 (top), 104, 107, 108, 110 (left), 111, 112, 116, 119; Metro-Goldwyn-Mayer, 91, 102, 115; Metro-Goldwyn-Mayer/United International Pictures, 115; National Film Archive, 20 (bottom), 27, 39, 50, 65, 91, 96, 98, 102, 103 (bottom), 114, 115, 120 (right), 124 (left), 127, 134 (bottom), 135, 136 (top), 137, 143, 150, 154, 156, 157, 158 (top left), 159, 160 (bottom), 161 (right), 162, 164, 169, 174, 175 (bottom); National General Pictures, 127 (left); Orion Pictures/Warner Bros. 157, 162; Pacific Films Limited, 175 (bottom); Paramount Pictures, 114, 122 (bottom), 124 (left); Particam Pictures, 95; Penthouse Film International, 154 (top); Otto Preminger, 103 (bottom); The Rank Organisation plc, 39 (bottom), 50, 96; Geoff Reeve Pictures Limited, 170, 173, 177 (bottom); Houston Rogers, courtesy Theatre Museum, London, 48, 52, 54; Shakespeare Centre Library, Stratford-upon-Avon, 42, 45; Thames Television Limited, 158 (bottom), 171; Theatre Museum, London, 31, 33; John Timbers, 131; The Times Newspapers Limited, 1, 40, 41, 51, 58, 67, 109, 115, 123, 139; Twentieth Century-Fox, 134 (bottom), 164; United Artists, 98; Universal Pictures Limited, 157; John Vickers Archive, 15; Warner Bros, 65; Wheel Productions, 158 (top left); Woodfall Films, 120 (right); Zespol Filmowy, 166.

The author would like to add a personal note of thanks to: Anita Appel, Lydia Cullen, Jeannie Donovan, Gillian Edwards-Jones, Sheila Formoy and H.M. Tennent Ltd, Peter and Jenny Hanna, Peter Hirst, Jane Judge, Don Mead, Marjorie Pepe, Alison Rogers, Jonathan Vickers, Mary White, and everybody at the BFI stills and reference library.

INDEX